CAPTURING
FREEDOM'S CRY
Arab Women Unveil Their Heart

GHADA SAMMAN

Translated by Rim Zahra, Ph.D. and Razzan Zahra, Ph.D.

BALBOA.
PRESS

A DIVISION OF HAY HOUSE

Originally published in Arabic by Ghada Al-Samman Press:
I'tikal Lahzah Haribah (Capturing a Fleeting Moment), 1979

Balboa Press books may be ordered through booksellers or by contacting:

Balboa Press
A Division of Hay House
1663 Liberty Drive
Bloomington, IN 47403
www.balboapress.com
1 (877) 407-4847

Print information available on the last page.

ISBN: 978-1-9822-1778-5 (sc)
ISBN: 978-1-9822-1780-8 (hc)
ISBN: 978-1-9822-1779-2 (e)

Library of Congress Control Number: 2018914594

Balboa Press rev. date: 05/10/2019

"Life is a bubble, capture it before it explodes."

An expression written on the door
of a photographer in Najaf, Iraq

"How can you make a microsecond last forever?"

From a magazine camera advertisement *

CONTENTS

Tribute to Ghada Samman xi

Translators' Note. xiii

~~Dedication~~ Dedication Withdrawn. xvii

Capturing a Petrified Fish. 1

Capturing a Rainbow? 2

Capturing Two Heads with One Bullet! 4

Capturing Straw in a Sweater's Sleeve 7

Capturing a Night of Sobbing for 99 Lebanese Qirush. 9

Capturing Poorly Read Words 14

Capturing Tremors of Oppression. 15

Capturing a Moment's Detour 17

Capturing a Moment's Fear 18

Capturing a Lie in a Moment's Honesty 20

Capturing a Martyred Moment 21

Releasing a Captured Moment... 23

Capturing the Princess of Beggars. 27

Capturing an Echo 28

Capturing Claws Hidden in a Furry Hand! 29

Assassinating a Fleeting Moment 32

Capturing a Gasp of the Heart 36

Capturing a Telephone Call! 37

Capturing a Bloody Moment! 41

Capturing a Drop of Colored Rain 43

Capturing an Ocean of Jealousy! 47

Capturing Unheard Voices 48

Capturing Sweetness That Escaped War! 50

Capturing Love (A Telex)! 52

Capturing a Satanic Memory! 54

Capturing a Tender Touch 56

Capturing a Gun! 57

Capturing a Moment of Choking 59

Capturing Certainty 61

The Old Woman Captures Her Wedding 63

Capturing a Moment of Optimism 65

Capturing an Evening on the Beach! 67

Capturing R.F. * 69

A Fleeting Moment Captures Me 70

Capturing an Argument 72

Capturing Telepathy 73

Capturing the Parachute of a Dream 74

Capturing a Question Mark!. 76

Capturing Beginnings of a Breakup 77

Capturing a Lost Kiss. 80

Capturing a Fairy Tale 82

Capturing a Pierced Memory 83

Capturing a Moment of Vulnerability. 85

Capturing Punishment. 86

Capturing a Lusty Moment 87

Capturing a Flying Beak! 89

Capturing the Murderer and the Murdered!. 91

Capturing the Arriving Man. 94

Capturing the Cries of Screams without Mouths 96

Capturing My Scattered Remains. 98

Capturing a Moment's Longing 100

Capturing a Book's Dedication. 102

Capturing a Fleeting Melody 103

Capturing Birds That Morph into Monkeys. 105

Capturing the Word "Masculinity" 107

Capturing Nostalgia 108

Capturing a Gasp 109

Capturing Another Orbit 110

Capturing Contradiction 112

Capturing 13 Owls 114

Capturing an Eye Resisting a Chisel... (The Eye Always Resists the Chisel...) 115

Capturing a Moment of Health 119

Capturing an Explosion 120

Capturing Fear (In a Rose Garden Sanitized with Alcohol) 122

Capturing Disappointment Disguised as Wisdom 124

Capturing a Window 125

Capturing a Corpse beneath the Lines 126

Capturing a Moment of Pain 128

Capturing a Small Earthquake 130

Capturing a Moment of Humiliation 131

Ghada Samman: A Biographical Sketch 133

Works Cited 143

Translators' Acknowledgment 147

Translators' Biographies 149

TRIBUTE TO GHADA SAMMAN

As she says it herself, she's "the queen of madness, freedom, challenge, and love... love...." Ghada Samman, whose novels are internationally known, unveils herself in these poems which are a long cry in the night we're traversing. She's a fierce fighter. Her first struggle is her life-long struggle to be, and to remain, free. Now, her poetic voice transcends styles, every line a double liberation: from literary conventions, and from the social ones. She reaches an unbelievable intimacy, takes us into the secrets "of a modern soul which is in the body of a Neanderthal." Then, when a war happens, she, who sees war as a challenge to freedom, lives the catastrophe fully, interweaving it with her experiment of love: they seem to feed on each other and make her poems reach the density of some of the Sufi writings. She holds nothing back, the terror created by war being equal to the one, or the ones, created by her diverse encounters with love. She turns to poetry in order to follow the thread of her life, to seek light in chaos. She finds in the confrontation between love and war a kinship, an affinity, I would say, an ethics. But, on her way, she definitely doesn't look for appeasement, but rather makes explode all the rules, those of poetry, and those of the social world. Like Heraclitus, she says "Being is strife." Free to the end, passionate to the end, she lives fully all contradictions and gives us a masterpiece which reflects masterly, like no one else, the jungle she has been and the jungle she is. Dear Ghada, you redeem unknowingly war, and love.

Etel Adnan
American-Lebanese poet, novelist, and visual artist

Translators' Note

Originally published in 1979 by the Ghada Al-Samman Press in Beirut, Lebanon, *Capturing Freedom's Cry: Arab Women Unveil Their Heart* is Ghada Samman's earliest poetry collection to address the Lebanese Civil War (1975-1990). Written during the early phase of the conflict, these poems lay bare the chaotic horror of war and place women at its destructive center.

Samman made a deliberate initial choice to stay in Lebanon, and even when she moved to France in 1985 with her husband Bashir Al-Daouq and only child, Hazim, she maintained her home and her press in Beirut. The poems provide a critical insider's experience of the early war years. In the original Arabic text, Samman dates each of her poems as a way to document her own day-to-day response to the war around her, and we have, therefore, placed these dates after each of the poems.

The original Arabic title of the book is *I'tikal Lahzah Haribah* or *Capturing a Fleeting Moment*. We changed the title of the book upon Samman's request in order to make clear that the poems are centered on the experience of Arab women. Although readers in the Arab world would readily associate Samman's work with gender equality and Arab women's rights, a Western audience would not necessarily draw that connection from the original title of the book.

This translation is not strictly literal, though we have striven to closely adhere to the meaning, in all its richness, of the text. We sought to capture the essential meaning of Samman's poems by very frequently retaining her verse structure, her similes, metaphors, images, repetitive echoes, and above all, her tone, her attitude toward her material. Translation is a journey through compromise, and we traveled and retraveled its paths by continually referring back to the text and rereading our translation aloud to listen for coherence, emphasis, and the voice within the poem.

Occasional compromises were inevitably made. As Robert Frost aptly puts it, "Poetry is what gets lost in translation." Indeed, it is impossible to move a poem wholly from one language to another, from one culture to another, one time to another no matter how competent the translator is in both languages. Our primary purpose has, therefore, been to save all we can and to do so out of a deep love of the original and a wish to bring Samman's unique and remarkable use of language, her feminism, and her deep exploration of intimate human relationships to a new, English-speaking audience.

Last, a note about the ellipses, which are a key feature of Samman's style and which have no parallels in standard English poetry: We chose to keep the majority of them just where Samman placed them in the original text. In the poems, ellipsis functions as a literary device used to emphasize the importance of certain moments or indicate a trailing off to another thought or memory the poet is evoking. They provide the fleeting nature of reality that the poems seek to capture and which is referred to in the book's original title. Although ellipsis is usually associated with omission in English, Samman's intention when using it is not to indicate omitted events or thoughts but to follow their flow, their tenuous continuity, or to express the ultimate dissipation of thought or experience into infinity. In this book's war-time setting, ellipses are particularly effective in expressing the sudden explosions of violence and the shock to perception, the loss and longing for lost values, attachments, and order, the attack upon hope and love, and the cry for freedom of the individual.

More technically, the use of ellipsis sets Samman's style apart in that it does not follow the symmetrical and classical forms of Arabic poetry or *qasīda*. Samman adopts a modern approach to Arabic poetry that is more flexible in its expression of experience and time. Ellipsis gives a new rhythmical sense to her poems, filling them with slow-moving spaces, and moves them away from the accepted metrical systems of classical Arabic poetry. Samman also ends some poems with an exclamation or question mark followed by an ellipsis, something that has no equivalent at all in English. This use of ellipsis suggests that, even though the memories and desires expressed in the poem have come to an emphatic or questionable end, they will continue to echo and flow in time or into timelessness. Lastly, Samman rarely uses periods to end a thought or a stanza. We, however, bowing to English expectation, often, though not always, chose to use capital letters—not present in Arabic—and periods to mark sentence structure because we felt that their absence would lead to confusion and that their insertion would aid in the presentation, coherence, and organization of ideas within the poems.

We would like to conclude with a thought central to the nature of the book. Embedded within many of the poems is a woman's voice that expresses an unyielding sense of hope, of determination to persevere and see Lebanon, and by extension, all war-torn countries, return to peace. And it is our sincere hope that our translation is successful in conveying the strength and vision Samman instilled in her poetry.

DEDICATION
DEDICATION WITHDRAWN

I cannot dedicate
this book to you…my love…
Its brilliant moments escape far
to places I do not know…

I cannot dedicate to you what I don't possess…
If I do, it'll be like someone giving a star running in space
or a storm or a wave or lightning and thunder
or a volcano
infinite…infinite…infinite space…

I cannot dedicate to you these fleeting moments…
If I do, I'd be like someone giving fish
from the Mediterranean to a corpse on the beach…

Ghada Samman

Capturing a Petrified Fish

You gave me a 40 million-year-old petrified fish…
and said, "This is one of a kind.
The ocean fell in love with her
and so made her immortal!"

***

But don't you see as I do:
The moment the ocean captured the fish with his love,
he also killed her!…

***

Art alone
may succeed in capturing a fleeting moment
without killing it,
or dying with its death…

12/14/1976
This poem has been translated into Farsi.

Capturing a Rainbow?

I love you,
but I refuse to let you entrap me,
just as a river refuses to be confined
to a narrow stream...

***

Be a waterfall or a lake,
be a cloud or a dam...
my water will gush through the stony grip of your waterfall
and continue its course.
I will gather in your lake
and keep on gushing...
One day your dam will imprison me for some time,
but my waters will overflow or explode...
My waters may evaporate, your cloud may imprison me,
but it will rain— I will be free
to return to my original springs...

***

I love you,
but you cannot imprison me,
just like a waterfall cannot trap a river.
The lake and cloud fail,
and so does the dam...
So love me as I am: a fleeting moment...
accept me as I am,
be the ocean,

be vast like the ocean,
be deep like the ocean,
so I may flow into you freely!...

***

You say I'm mercury, quicksilver—
I cannot be contained...
...but before mercury formed...
it was love's glint in a woman's eye.
Her lover, a scientist, tried to capture
and freeze her gaze, turn it into hard metal,
but instead, mercury was formed!...

***

Don't you see, my darling, that raisins
are a poor attempt to capture a fleeting grape?

***

So, love me as I am.
Don't try to capture my gaze or my soul.
Accept me as I am,
just as the ocean accepts all the rivers that flow into it,
so that they run toward it eternally...
Despite the waterfalls, dams, and lakes,
the rivers know how to find their way
into the ocean's infinite embrace...

1/1/1975
This poem has been translated into Farsi

Capturing Two Heads
with One Bullet!

The electricity is dead,
the lamps are broken
like eyes popped out of their sockets.
The corpses of wires lie scattered over the asphalt,
the asphalt turned into rubble by bombs
(missiles 120 and 155…cannons 75 and 82).
When I twist my ankle on the sidewalk's pit,
I hear that unforgettable sound all over again
(the sound of missiles exploding).
I relive the scene of people dying,
my fear for them, my relief that I am not them!…

***

The night is grieving, yet cautious—
the streets are empty except for rats,
terror, and dismembered bodies,
along with armor, dreams, and prayers.
The windows are emptied of everything
except the ghosts living inside mourning dresses
that hang on balcony clotheslines to dry…

***

We walk in the streets
beneath the ghostly moonlight…
In that scary scene,
I lean on you,

I feel your branches of tenderness
reach out to me…

In the ghostly moonlight,
you transformed into a tribe of men,
all the men I had loved,
all the men I would love
later on—when we meet…

***

We walk…
traffic signs hang over corpses,
street lights are melted,
and the gazes of the few passersby are
like sharp spears exchanging mutual terror…
My hand hides in yours,
you envelop me
like an eyelid protecting the eye in a storm…

***

It is war,
the moon's light descends like a curtain of horror,
spreading itself over the dying…
Death trembles in fear…
Beirut's terrorized streets
run beneath our feet…

***

When my head came close to yours,
we could hear hundreds of weapons
being loaded, hundreds of bullets being fired
by anxious fingers.

We clung to each other so close...
that one bullet would have been enough
for both our heads.
So, is it love or fear that glues us together?...

10/7/1976
This poem has been translated into Farsi.

Capturing Straw
in a Sweater's Sleeve

Who will dare to lift the curtain,
knowing that the moon is waiting behind it
to wake up longing for those faraway?
(I wonder where you are now...
I wonder, do you see the moon?)...

***

Who will dare to wear last winter's sweater
that has a piece of straw caught in its sleeve,
carrying memories of the afternoon
we lay together on Hyde Park's grass?
This is the straw that broke forgetfulness' back...

***

Who will dare to lie in bed,
knowing the memory of laughter,
in the same bed,
will climb over your feet like a beanstalk
and gather over your chest like a gravestone?

***

Who will dare to reach
into last winter's coat pocket,
knowing they'll find an old cinema ticket
that reminds them of the precious hand they held
in that beautiful fleeting moment?...

***

Does the person whose love is as honest as death
dare to reprimand the one whose love is
an earthly terrain?...

10/7/1977

Capturing a Night of Sobbing for 99 Lebanese Qirush

I will not forget crying alone
in the parking lot
on that salty night
when I paid 99 qirush* to find
a vacant space where I could silently inhale
and look for another path…

***

I remember that night of crying
in the parking lot…
the night was a continent of loss.
Moments ago,
I had left your pirate body,
the ocean, my lifeboat,
and the parking lot drowned.
I knew cold, and I knew heat,
but I didn't know warmth…

***

I left the deceit, the mercury eyes,
I loved the deceit, the mercury eyes,
your hunter's body dying in legendary tales.
I loved you,
I loved the dream of a bridge
between my soul and your rowdy chaos…

---

* A "qirsh" (plural "qirush") is a coin of small value. The Lebanese pound is made
up of 100 qirush. High inflation during the Lebanese Civil War eliminated this
subdivision.

I loved you—in my darkest hours—
as if you were the earth's last swallow...

***

That night of crying for 99 qirush
in the parking lot...
I remember feeling how your neck, vigorous,
pulsating, was surrounded by a necklace
made from the teeth of all the women
who loved you!...

***

That night of crying for 99 qirush,
I thought to talk to you about love,
but when you talked to me about the body,
your pupils disappeared
and your eyes transformed into mirrors,
reflecting light sharp as a dagger's edge...

***

That night of crying for 99 qirush,
I finally realized that you
still live in the time of coffee shops,
and I live in the time of forests...

***

That night of crying for 99 qirush,
memories swept over me
of our rusted past,
and I knew the depth of my love for you—

you, the one so satisfied with curtains
and stolen kisses in a winter-dark car...

***

In the parking lot
for 99 qirush...
I loved you with a love as wide as the dawn,
as loud as a riot...
When you held my hand,
my fingers became green branches,
blossoming with bird melodies.
Whenever we met,
love uttered a sigh of relief...

***

That night of crying for 99 qirush
in the parking lot...
I staggered into the last field of sadness,
one more step, I would've fallen
off the planet.
The parked cars stared at me with their silent, shut-off eyes,
surrounded me like a tribe of robots
whose batteries were run down by grief.
I was shattered glass.
The walls echoed my
screaming silence...

***

That night of crying for 99 qirush,
I remembered how the two of us made plans for all seasons:
winter, spring, summer, fall.

I shouted at you,
Over there is the season of bleeding
and there is the season of drought.
Over there is the season of parting
and there is the season of death...
What are we going to do with all these seasons?

But you didn't hear me...
and I stood like someone bleeding
in front of a closed door.

***

That night of crying for 99 qirush,
I dove deep into my bones,
remembering the glorious torture
of being with you, my fall
into your shifting sands,
how you passed through my life
like the shadow of a plane
flying over a dry field.
When I let go of your hand that night
without even saying *goodbye...*
I knew I was a ship drowning
into oceans of despair...

***

That night of crying for 99 qirush,
the boy working at the parking lot asked,
"Why are you still here?"
I replied, *I'm out of gas, my brother.*
So, naively, he ran to get me some...

What gas could ignite a woman you've turned into salt,
dissolving beneath night's waterfall,
a woman who knows that...without you...
she'll disappear like a face in a mirror
after the candle is blown out?!...

4/7/1977

Capturing Poorly Read Words

Let the artery continue to pulse
between presence and absence, hanging
on the fences of night…anticipating…

***

Let the dream continue to be pure
as falling snow on a cornfield,
so it cannot be stepped on
by the dirty feet of reality…

***

I don't want love,
I want a dream…
I don't want a body,
I want a shadow...

***

Does this poem mean anything to you?
Or are you like all the rest—you're going to read it
without reading me?…

A fall-like spring 1977
This poem has been translated into Farsi

14

Capturing Tremors of Oppression

I talked to you about my love,
not knowing that I was whistling
to a wandering bird…

***

I told you that you can't take back a bullet,
once it's fired.
I told you my love is not a public bench
that you can sit on and leave as you please…

***

Over and over, I said love's gown
is as delicate as butterfly wings…
Rip it, and there can be no needle of forgiveness…

***

I warned you against
fooling around with your axe
in love's forest…
The trees forever remember every beautiful word…
and every wound…every wound…
you cut into their bark.

***

But you didn't believe that my velvet heart
can turn into steel,
that my springs—exploding at your feet—

15

can turn into fiery cactus
with thorns poisonous to the touch...
And that the word "goodbye" simply means: "Goodbye!!"

4/2/1976

Capturing a Moment's Detour

I arm myself with my books,
my philosophers, and historians…
I run from your rough hands
to the softness of my records…
I climb up the ladders of Beethoven
and hide my trembling body
under one of his notes…

***

I protect myself from your simple logic
with Hellenistic philosophy,
the memory of museums,
statues, paintings,
and the millions of ancient columns
I've seen…

***

But you step into my life
and bloody earthquakes follow your footsteps.
Your body is a tornado…
you tear my books with your storm…
and they fly from the windows of my soul
like feathers of mummified birds…
You burn my art and music
—My ruins collapse—

***

In the midst of this turbulent night,
you reach for me…I surrender…at dawn's rising.

9/3/1976

Capturing a Moment's Fear

Is it possible for the dream ship
to sail out of the shallows
where social life is a trivial chess game,
and can it sail twice?

***

Is it possible for a bird,
caught in the sticky lies of social duty,
to resume its joyful migration?

***

Is it possible for happiness
to blossom on the tree of nostalgia
twice in one season of sadness?

***

Is it possible for our lips, wet with blood
—each washed with the other's blood—
to smile again?...

***

Is it possible for our broken love
to mend without cracking again?...

***

Is it possible for the star of love
to return to its place in the sky?...

***

Maybe not...
but because I truly love you,
we will bathe in the same river twice!...*

9/14/1976

---

* Samman is referring to the Greek philosopher Heraclitus' famous line, "No man ever steps in the same river twice, for it's not the same river and he's not the same man." *From: https://www.goodreads.com/quotes/117526-no-man-ever-steps-in-the-same-river-twice-for*

Capturing a Lie
in a Moment's Honesty

Love is my favorite lie…
it numbs me to life's details and nonsense…and explodes me…

***

I choose love,
but don't care much about choosing the man…
It's not important what man I love,
it's important to remain in a state of love…

***

Since time always ticks as loud
as the firing of bullets, I know:
Every moment could be the last,
every moment that passes is unique,
precious…
And because I can't stop time,
I pounce on love and devour it!

***

Since there is no tomorrow for us,
let's savor our love's entirety
in one day, far away
from procrastination's
empty rules…

2/2/1975
This poem has been translated into Farsi.

20

Capturing a Martyred Moment

...The moon was pale,
the ocean cried for help,
my heart, a car wailing
in dark and abandoned streets...
The sidewalks shrieked,
hens cackled,
cats yowled,
and dogs gasped in terror
of an approaching catastrophe...

***

And *they* were watching you...my love...

***

On that night, my prayers were your pillow,
my dream dressed your wound.
I washed your face with the blood of our unborn children...

***

When the militiaman passed you by the first time,
he thought you were a spike of wheat...
When he passed you by the second time,
he thought you were a candle...
When he passed you by the third time,
he thought you were an axe...

***

He grasped the axe,
cut the wheat,
blew the candle,
not knowing that it would turn into dynamite!

8/31/1976
This poem has been translated into Farsi.

Releasing a Captured Moment…

Where's our ocean cave?
The coffins of those days
stand still in darkness, side by side
like sealed postal packages.

A rattling snake hisses at the lost memories
of our village, abolished by those mercenaries…

I'll never forgive you
for letting them
destroy our ocean cave,
our temple filled with incense and music…

***

Where's our water?
My mouth is torn by the word "goodbye"…
The springs are dry…

I gave you the only cup of water remaining
in the city of leprosy…
You threw it on the ground,
and I thanked you.

***

Where's our lighthouse?
How could you turn your eyes away
when the mercenaries were stealing our days,
devouring our memories and our unborn children?

***

23

Where are the legends?
Have they become the mere stories of old folk
in nursing homes, smoking
a hookah filled with blood?

***

Where is the forest in the village of Aramoun?*
After the third turn,
and by the fifth tree,
you'll find my bones and silver jewelry—
I've been dead for a year.

***

Do you remember the night we parted?
You asked for the impossible—
you told me to stand naked against a wall
and let time flagellate me until I bled
and passed out.

***

When we argued that night,
we were not enemies,
but disputing with fate...
We ignored that and attacked
each other instead.

***

Sadness poured over our last day together...
We drank it like aged wine

---

* Samman may be referring to Aramoun, a village located in the Alley District in
the Mount Lebanon Governorate of Lebanon. This area houses mainly a Drouz
community, and due to the religious nature of the Civil War, the village became a
battleground during the years 1975-1990.

—so we became more alert—
we licked our sadness from the trees, streets,
and car windows that passed us by.
In vain, rain's transparent tongue tried to wipe it
from the face of our last day…

***

That night,
I inhaled heavily in your arms,
a fish in love with its bait.

When the sun rose, Parting came and ripped me
from your chest like a flagellator…
he took me to the airport
where he hung me on the wing of a plane.

***

Where is our laughter?
It's in the remaining bones of a white whale
that swam in search of a transparent dream
and continued to swim in the sand, drowning
in a mirage pool.

***

Where are our nights?
Abandoned corpses
on streets decayed by bullets.

***

Where are you?
You're as close as my skin

25

and as far as memories
of my mother's womb.

***

Where is our love?
It runs barefoot in the forests
with long hair and nails,
and no memories!...

5/27/1976

Capturing the Princess of Beggars

The images are all mixed up
and I lost my face.
You were my mirror that broke
as I was climbing those rough mountains
on my way to you.

**

You used to call me, "Princess…princess of beggars…"
But I was also the hungry princess of a damned heart,
the princess of nostalgia crazed with longing,
the princess of love that is black in all its whiteness,
the princess of burnt grass,
the princess of broken trees…

**

My ambition was to love you,
so I could continue to be aware of our unborn children's coming,
so I could remember the days and the names of months
along with all the silly idioms
existing on our funny planet…

**

Here you are running away from my frantic world.
Here I am riding again on my broom,
flying over the mountains, the valleys, and the centuries
to search for you…to lose you…

4/6/1977

Capturing an Echo

The echo
is a dead man
who is unavenged.

***

The echo is a murdered man whose final cry
was not heard—the will.

***

The echo
is a continuation of life,
an artery crossing over the illusion of death.

***

The echo is your silent cry as the bullet
goes through your body...
                    —I step over it
and walk toward that golden bird of joy
we used to chase together before they hunted you down!
I will keep on trying...

Undated in original Arabic text

Capturing Claws Hidden
in a Furry Hand!

Soon, the pearls of light will stop dancing
over the mercury ocean...The sun will leave and with it
our afternoon of wanton love...

***

I relax under the sun,
licking yesterday's wounds,
waiting for tomorrow's...
I surrender to the peace of the moment,
the relief between one stab and the next.
I've mastered the lessons of your love...
I've learned not to be completely attached to you
—so you don't get bored with me—
and not to get so unattached that you forget me...

***

I've mastered how to touch
your love—a minefield...
holding tight explodes it,
a loose hold keeps it ignited.
I've learned to surrender my days,
my ravenous emotions, my volcanoes
to calm your hellish love.
I've made our longing the twin of rejection,
our meetings synonymous with a little parting...

***

I've built dams
around my love's springs…
The whips of self-restraint
lash the back of my longing…
I've learned that, with you, excess only leads to scarcity,
that you don't want me to give you my love,
you want me to give you the thrill of stealing it!…

***

Before this,
I would scream in your face, *I love you!*
And you'd respond with cold silence…
Now,
I choke the cry, *I love you*
inside my heart…
(my cries are like the beating of ancient drums in an African forest).
I strangle the words, *I love you*
under my skin…
I torment you with cold silence,
secretly enjoying your tormented cry, "I love you!"

***

The moment my love became a field of spring roses,
wildly blooming from deep within me,
I gave you all my spontaneous madness
and outpouring joy…
—that very moment, you refused me!

***

Today,
my love for you is a single, black, legendary rose
in a snowy field fenced by thorns,
poisonous as the fangs of snakes…

And here you are spending your day
running around the fence,
calling my name...
I can no longer turn back
into a wild field of spring flowers...
You can no longer pick a single flower
from my heart's snowy hills...

***

The sun is setting,
falling deep into the clouds...
The pearls of light stop dancing over the ocean...
yet a line of light sneaks from the pile of clouds,
thin, delicate, sharp like a sword...

***

My love for you was like a shepherd's love,
your love for me resembled that of philosophers and geniuses.
Here I am continuing
my journey towards keeping the hellish balance
of your love's mysteries...
So, don't blame me,
if on some sunny morning you ask,
"Do you love me?"
And I say, *yes and no*!

1/11/1976

Assassinating a Fleeting Moment

Here I am again
in that crazy night world…
where there are burning faces of strangers
with their incomprehensible murmurs around cups of forgetfulness…
the agitated music,
and the loud laughter from the soul's secret pains.

***

Here I am again
in that crazy night world…
escaping from the barricades of your love,
its minefields…
I throw myself against bright streams of madness,
so I can assassinate
your daily executions of me…

***

Here I am again
in the madness of dance and forgetfulness…
among young men with faces like Christ,
eyes staring at all the other eyes,
searching for a refuge, a roof, a star…and a bullet
for obstinate Time—a monster that stands on the doorstep
devouring anyone who dares to abandon it…

***

Here I am again,
entering the climate of cruelty…
truly beginning the journey of my estrangement from you,

leaning on the arm of another man I will love
—I don't know his name yet—

***

I suffer (a little) for you...
We watched the clouds together,
you and I.
We watched the mountains,
we touched the grass,
and we listened to rain falling.
We cried together, we lost our minds together,
we even died together on the nights of our souls' estrangement.
And now, we're assassinating all of it?

***

Here I am again
in that crazy night world...
I write your name in ink on a cigarette,
smoke it, and watch your name burn away,
letter
by
letter.
I exhale you towards the iron ceiling...
I write your unforgettable phone number on a cigarette,
smoke it, and watch the fire eat away the numbers
one
by
one...
I shoot a bullet of silence into each.
—Ah, dying grief burns.

If I were in a forest,
I would beat the drums
and howl like legendary wolves

33

at the full moon.
I'd paint my face
with the blood of wild blueberries.
But I'm here,
leaning on the arm of a man I will love
—I didn't ask his name—
dying grief will not allow me to ask yet…
my only protest is to dance in tears.

***

Ah, my longing for you
is a sharp pain…
our days come to me like the sands of a desert wave…
its pebbles bruise me…
it carries me into your arms,
then returns me to the night's ocean
inside the music-box of chaotic forgetfulness.

Oh Night, Night, Night
draw out my tears like a black leech,
but be careful not to exhale my grief
because the knives will gather around
a sheep that (has fallen) in love,
rather than a sheep that (has stood up) in love…

***

Here I am again
in that crazy night world…
flirting with a man I don't know
—but will love.
I suffer and feel
the noblest part of my being die.
I transform into a woman I don't know…

If we ever meet again,
you wouldn't recognize me either...

***

But I dream of spring flowers
growing on the edge of my wound,
just as I watched them this morning blooming
at the edge of a pit
hollowed by a missile...
It's as if each flower was assassinating
the moments of explosion...and destruction...

5/5/1977

Capturing a Gasp of the Heart

Is that really you?
I look at you,
I search for you inside of you,
but I can't find you!...

***

Where did you go
without leaving?...
How did you leave
without going?...

***

I see your eyes, your lips, your arms,
your body,
but where are you?
Ah, how I miss you.
Where are you?

***

I loved in you the scent not the flower,
the pulse not the body...
I loved the rustle of the wind in your leaves,
not the wooden bark.
I loved in you the dream...the dream...
        the dream...
How could you murder it?...

8/17/1977
This poem has been translated into Farsi.

Capturing a Telephone Call!

"Guess who it is…" I recognized it:
your voice coming out of a suitcase,
thrown onto the edge of my handset,
ricocheting into my heart's wound.

***

I recognized it:
your voice…but I didn't dare utter your name…
I was surprised…scared…
as often happens
when last night's dream becomes a reality…

***

I've seen you in my dreams every night
since you gazed into my eyes…that satanic gaze!…
Your face glowed with evil radiance
and devious innocence.

***

What curse threw you into my hell?
What curse can get you out of my hell?
Was it a coincidence that we first met at an airport
and parted as passersby on fast trains heading in opposite directions?

***

When we met, your love dragged me into the night
and it still refuses to set me free…

***

We parted, but I still hear your voice…
a future memory…it whispers
like a soothsayer's prophecy…
"I'll see you, I'll hear you, and I'll love you…"
I decided, no one can torture you but me…
Is this what it means to love you?
I don't know…
But I waited for you
like a lonely tree on an island, dreaming of a castaway
it can hold prisoner…

***

That brief encounter at the airport—I screamed silently
when they announced your plane's departure…
Give me your heart and follow me,
give me your wounds and follow me,
give me your body and follow me,
for my heart is grieving and the night is long…
If you touch me, I will bloom like a tree
caressed by spring's fingertips…
and I will ignite like white flowers.
You said goodbye with deadly silence,
a silence of steel and the burning cold of ice.
Your lips were as merciless as a tsunami sent from afar…
You whispered, "Only I'll see you, I'll hear you, and I'll love you."
I didn't whisper, *I don't want anyone to torture you but me!*
You left like a straying wind
and you pierced through my heart
like a fog that never lifts…

***

"Guess who it is…"
I pretend I don't know
that you are the one I want no one to torture but me!

***

"You never asked about me..."
I asked about you…my darling…
all the addresses I knew...
all the night hotels…the bars…the boardwalk…the sailboats…
I waited for you at the ocean.
I waited beneath the ocean's rains.
My head beat like a heart.
I expected to see you
walk into my life (against traffic).

***

I asked the ocean's dawn about you,
the seagulls circling for food,
the fish below, the seashells, the corals, even the snails.
I asked the creatures caught in fishermen's nets.
I searched for your footsteps
on the sand by the ebbs and flows.
I cried out to you…
>   *Happy is the woman that has a couch in your heart.*
>   *O you invader of my body,*
>   *the one who ties banners around my nerves,*
>   *plants flags over my body's landscape and longing…*
>   *O you roaming my nights like a vampire…*
>   *Everyone I ever knew before you*
>   *built my city's gates—now open to you—*
>   *rock by rock,*
>   *door by door,*
>   *lock by lock…*
>   *You're far away and near,*
>   *invisible and yet transparent.*
>   *My city gates are waiting for you*
>   *to open them like a prince in a fairy tale…*

***

I didn't try to forget that encounter
on airplane wings…
Forget you?
That's like trying to dig a tunnel through a mountain
with only a needle…

***

I waited for you…
I asked the rusted iron
along Beirut's Corniche* about you.
I read your name written on seaweed deep in the ocean.
I called for you…
I loved you with an untamed love that grew and spread
like a carnivorous plant.
Waiting, I screamed your name from the abyss
and from the water's surface.
I waited for you,
a loyal peasant, a fragile wound.
Trembling from a love that would not die, I screamed,
No one will torture you but me!

***

When your voice comes to me,
whispering like colored dust…I decide:
From this day on, no woman will torture you but me!…

5/2/1977

---

* The Corniche is a wide sidewalk or promenade in Beirut's Central District. It
  overlooks the ocean and is surrounded by palm trees with bullet holes in them. A
  popular location for tourists and locals before and after the Lebanese Civil War, the
  Corniche is usually crowded with people jogging, running, strolling, biking, and
  roller blading. There are also pushcart vendors that offer passersby coffee, juice,
  soft drinks, hot chestnuts, and other snacks.

Capturing a Bloody Moment!

O brave one,
were you fighting or committing suicide
when you raised your spear in one hand
and called for a cease-fire with the other?

***

That day we said: *In order to live,*
a few of us must get killed
and a few must kill...

***

O brave one,
all matters of the heart
have now slid into the caves of forgetfulness
—except your image the moment you exploded—
memory became sealed
by the burns of raging blood...

***

Because you whispered without a voice
—the moment you exploded—
your words echoed in my ear like thunder:
Have mercy on the flagellators of prostitutes
and adulterers—and mercy upon death—
For the love of life...don't betray my dream...

***

I won't betray the dream of childhood innocence and joy,
I won't betray all those corpses tired of being slaughtered
and longing for rebirth...

***

Today I say: *In order to live,*
a lot of us must get killed
and a lot of us must kill...

7/7/1976

Capturing a Drop
of Colored Rain

I exhale you…
and reclaim my lungs…
I'm leaving your snowfields and ashes.
I lift my broken eyelashes toward the horizon
and wait for a new hope
to rise in my body…

***

I exhale you…
For a long time, I believed
you were my only love,
that you were the source of all joy…
I vowed: *I testify there is no love but yours…**
without realizing I was delivering my heart to its tomb!…

***

I exhale you…
You slit my throat with your arrogance,
tore me to pieces…and scattered my remains
across dark hills…
Forgetfulness came…bent down to gather my bones…
and illuminated them…like a jellyfish…

***

---

* *I testify there is no love but yours* is a play on the Muslim principle of *shahada* (testifying): *la ilaha illa illah wa muhammad rasul allah*, meaning "There is no god but Allah and Muhammad is His prophet." Samman evokes *shahada* to expose gender stratification and to reveal how patriarchal society conditions women to position men as masters and gods.

I exhale you...
My memory, like a plow,
searches the destroyed lands
to find a wedge of truth
not yet ripped apart
by your earthquake...

***

I exhale you...
My inner voice cries, *escape,*
eclipsing all other voices...
escape ...escape ...escape ...
Shattered, I crawl out of your world's nightmare,
your toxic planet...
Ah, how did I manage to escape
before your sedative clouds swallowed me?

***

I exhale you...
The cold gathers outside my hotel window,
shadows dwell inside the darkness,
neutral and indifferent like the laughter of passersby...

***

I exhale you...
The distance between my wound and your arrogance
is a night of dying...
The distance between my cry and your ears
is a continent of indifference...
The distance between my head and yours

is a pillow of thorns...
And I'm sitting in my old place,
now completely empty of your presence...

***

I exhale you...
I gave you the reins of my soul,
but you tore me apart over an airplane wing...
and scattered me like colored rain in a lonely night...
Yet I continued to say:
Wherever you are, I will be with you,
wherever I am, you will stay with me...
until I lost my voice...

***

You never truly lived in the ocean,
you were living the game of power...
you were never innocent...like birds...
you were corrupt like all leaders and great-men...
you were never the beloved of birds and forests,
you were the beloved of power and possession...
you were never... you were never... you were never...

***

You left me no other choice...
I had to choose
between dying with you
or dying without you.
So, I chose to toss our time
into the continent of forgetfulness.
I had to save myself from you...

***

45

I exhale you...
and here I am once again flying alone,
here I am surrounded
        from the North by estrangement...
        from the South by estrangement...
        from the East by estrangement...
        from the West by estrangement...
I've thrown our time
into the continent of forgetfulness...

6/1/1976

Capturing an Ocean of Jealousy!

Your love was a golden flower,
bloodied with damnation...I sailed behind it
into an ocean, mysterious in its rough waters.
I left my head on the beach...

***

And when the seagulls
came to pluck my eyes,
they saw your image there
and they laughed a lot
with their orange and black beaks...
They whispered like old peasant women gossiping...
and they kept on with their mocking laughter.
They'd seen your image...my darling
in the eyes of dozens of beheaded women
scattered across the same beach!...

12/13/1977

Capturing Unheard Voices

Unheard voices speak
in unfamiliar tongues—
the scraping of fingernails on a blackboard,
the crackling of bones inside their ligaments
because of a dispute between the nerves...

***

The scraping of the violin's bow
over untuned strings,
squeaking unwritten notes
that haven't climbed the ladders of harmony,
but remain in the garden of silence...
while the violinist dies in silence...

***

The friction of language...inside an idea
shouting at the vocal cords...
The gasp of disbelief (unexhalable)
on a street where mummies roam.

***

Ah, those unheard voices
haven't yet been polished by time,
refuse to conform to the symmetry
of blood, vein, artery!

***

Ah, the cry of the modern soul
inside the body of a Neanderthal...
Ah, the piercing cry of an undiscovered alphabet
inside a fragile inherited language...

***

As in the cave, so in the street:
dinosaurs continue to jog
among skyscrapers...
without listening to the unheard voices ...

***

Go in peace,
but beware of feeling safe!...

Beirut~12/30/1977

Capturing Sweetness
That Escaped War!

The bombing has calmed,
the smell of gunpowder has faded.
We come out of our rooms—
the crickets, the mice, and us…

***

The ocean is vast, blue, serene.
The sunset is a pink wound
that spreads across the horizon…
Three palm trees, six clouds,
and a star stand in the distance.
The breeze is tender, nurturing
when you're near.
I feel you next to me and I'm happy
because you're still alive…
and I am too…and so is this beautiful planet…

***

Your presence is intense and magnetic,
profoundly tender…
All that I am pulsates with love for you
and never-ending gentleness…
All that I am is inhabited by peace
in your presence.

***

This evening is called:
the night of tenderness...gentleness...peace...
I can't believe the war is still going on.
Even the word "war" at this moment
has lost its meaning.

***

A bullet fires!
The sky rips!...
Hide me and hide inside me!!...

Beirut-8/24/1976
This poem has been translated into Farsi

Capturing Love (A Telex)!

Dear Mr. Businessman:
I'm not certain how to address you,
I don't have a calculator to use,
I don't have a checkbook (with a check)
to write on: I love you.

***

I understand that in your world,
the alphabet seems strange,
extinct like a flock of mythical rocs...
So I will write you (a telex) about love...

***

Let's try numbers...
Ten days have passed since we parted.
I won't tell you if I missed you
or not...
Ten days since your hand flew from mine
like an endangered bird...
Ten days?
Or should I say 864,000 seconds!
Is this any clearer?

***

Let's try numbers another way:
The world's population is 3 billion.
That is, 3,000 million people

and you're the only one of them I want to be with...
Is this any clearer?

***

Let's try numbers a different way:
Every minute on earth with you
equals 11 light years on some other planet
with anybody else...
One light year, dear sir,
equals 906 billion kilometers
and 11 light years equal
105,600,000,000 light steps,
a number equal to the wealth that you strive for...
Is this any clearer?

***

Dear Mr. Businessman:
Can you inform me
why the telex machine has just collapsed?

2/22/1975

Capturing a Satanic Memory!

I turn on the radio
but hear nothing...
I answer the phone
but don't know what I'm saying...
I read and can't comprehend...
I think of you, I conjure you...
and my cursed memory
can't forget a thing...

***

...Your body's hard as a rock,
your lips honey...

***

...Your eyes are cities of forgetfulness...
I shut myself inside...
doors without locks...
to lose myself for a while.

***

...Your eyelashes flicker like a possessed child
dancing to songs and prayers...
The smoke of your cigarette flows
like soothing music...

***

...Your caress has the flavor of a legend,
your breath a river's breeze,
you smell like tropical forests!...

Your beard is a magical cave,
your neck pulsates lust and loving tenderness...

***

...Your shoulders are sails
that can withstand stormy winds,
your arms strong as waterfalls,
your chest an endless beach,
I run on it with barefoot memories...

***

...Your waist is my hand's anchor,
your legs are stallions in forests of light...
Your back's a long river,
I sail on it to the springs of bliss.
Your mustache is an eagle's wing...
and I love the roc of Arab legend...
What else can I say?
I go back to the radio, the phone, and my book...
No use!
I can only conjure you again...
From the beginning...
I repeat...your body is a rock,
your lips honey...and...etc. ...

8/6/1976

Capturing a Tender Touch

Tenderness flows
without destination or goal...
Tenderness is a river of light,
running across time,
unconcerned with place...

***

Tenderness touches
concealed pain
on an unknown face
in a dark train...
with no one to applaud...or give anything in return.

8/19/1975

Capturing a Gun!

Dedicated to R.F., my friend (no longer with me),
who gave me a loaded gun with a note that read:
"To stop the bloodshed, this is the way."

You said, *This is the way.*
I ran across the borders of your vast wound,
stretching from your wounded pacific to your bleeding gulf,
from your pacific of memory to your destined gulf.
I know this path very well…
don't bother lighting candles…
believe me, I know this path
like a bird knows its migration route.
I've memorized the path of your arteries,
I've breathed your thunder
and made running against the traffic
inside your circulatory system my obsession.
I loved you as much as my hundred and fifty million paragraphs…

***

You said, *In order to stop the bloodshed: a gun…*
O gypsy of joy, teach me
how to sew up my wounds with your knife,
to patch the exploding sky with your thunder…
This is the way?
I once said it like you…
In that moment, death felt sweeter than falling rain.
Once, knowing used to light my soul
like a lighthouse inside lovers' eyes.
Once, I said it like you,
but they destroyed the trees on both sides of the street,
threw us into our water wells,

dug our tombs…and put mirrors inside of them…
They too said, *This is the way…*
I got lost in obstacles…and disappointments,
but I continued to love you
as much as my hundred and fifty million paragraphs…

***

Ah, friend of my wounds,
grant me a moment of faith
where my body is a gun and my throat a bullet.
Take me to the world of the extinct good people,
teach me how to forgive hypocrites
basking on the ocean's torn beaches.
Ah, friend of my wounds, teach me
how to load the holes in my soul with dynamite like you did…
show me how to protect myself from the thunder's winds,
to become the storm!…
I love you as much as my hundred and fifty million paragraphs…

8/30/1977

Capturing a Moment of Choking

My heart's fragile like a wound,
gloomy like muddied rain
in a remote train station...
Even voices hurt me...
even words of love
exhaust me...

Tonight, my heart's fragile like a wound,
all that I am longs for silence and serenity...
but people keep on talking just to make noise—
they gossip...gossip...
and can't shut up for a single moment.
Maybe they're afraid of hearing the voices deep within...
words...words...words...
flying into space
like a cloud of mosquitoes,
attacking and almost choking me...
I cannot breathe...
words...words...words...words...

***

Ah, human voices hurt me tonight...
If they would only shut up for a second,
they would hear the ocean waves,
the sound of sap running,
the sound of flowers blooming tonight,
crabs crawling on the sand,
the dialogue between the moon and the waves
in the game of ebb and flow...

and the sound of silence
inside a heart done with civilized crossword games
erroneously called conversations…

***

Ah silence,
I wish my lover were a fish,
swimming next to me in silence,
looking into my eyes in silence,
loving me in silence,
and leaving me in silence.

8/26/1977

Capturing Certainty

Glue yourself to me,
so I can believe my dream of you is still alive...
I can no longer shoulder Beirut's burden
without your love...
I can no longer bear streets furnished
with corpses, garbage, and flies.
Without your love, I can no longer bear seeing intestines
festering on Beirut's sidewalks.
How can I bear bullets suddenly firing for no reason
or youth strutting proudly with their guns
like models on fashion runways...

***

For a long time,
we stood in queues of humiliation
by the carts of bitter bread.
We heard the moans of the wounded lying
in front of hospital gates...the cries of children
hiding with rats, sharing crumbs and the dark.
How could I bear a city polluted by bleeding, pretense, and treachery
if I weren't waiting for the moment of your rising...

***

We stand on the summer sidewalks
like petrified trees,
among us those infected by cruelty...
their fingers are gun barrels.
Ambulances pass by
filled with bombs, not the wounded.

Ah, if it weren't for your love,
how could I bear the death of water,
the death of music,
the death of light,
and the death of all the voices, even the cries for help,
in this brutal, vicious city...

***

They will not steal my freedom.
They will not nail down my hooves.
They will not tie their bridles around my neck.
I will not be tamed by their atrocities,
I will not applaud the sound of the flagellators' whips
or claim—as everyone does—that it is the music of Beethoven.
I will continue to be capable of dreaming and flying
as long as I love you and wait for you,
knowing that your rising is inevitable.

Beirut-9/5/1976

The Old Woman Captures Her Wedding

The old woman
captures her fleeting wedding memories
with such naïve surreality
that it shocks her ancient bridal chest...

***

Here is her wedding dress, carefully wrapped
by time and moths...it's ragged and yellowed,
covered with the fingerprints of half a century...

***

Yet the old woman, rich and poor,
still opens her wedding chest
from time to time, continuously
for thousands of years...
She opens the box of her memories
and takes out her bundle,
and unwraps the dress that has changed
like her face and voice.
She notices the difference and she doesn't.

***

She holds the dress close to her body
and closes her eyes...
Her groom is dancing next to her
and inside the dress, she is young!...

***

Sensations of that time return to her,
its music and scents...
She shivers, feeling for a second,
the same forgotten joy...

5/22/1975

Capturing a Moment of Optimism

Winds can blow up a storm
and turn off the black candles
in a city of shattered lamps...

***

The ocean can erupt
and destroy all the lifeboats
that rescue lonely hearts...

***

A body of nostalgia can hold me in its arms
and drag me to a bed of snow and ashes...

***

Love can take off its mask
and reveal an old, deceptive face.
My lover can neglect me
like an old record he's tired of hearing...

***

Yet all of that cannot extinguish the embers
that forever burn deep inside me—
like the fire in the goddess' temple...

***

I've stumbled and fallen,
time after time...
My mountain has become an abyss,

my valley a swamp.
I've been burnt again and again…
I've watched the sun turn into a candle flame,
giants turn into dwarfs…
Yet none of that can extinguish the embers
that forever burn deep inside me…

***

I know the night is coming…
and I know it might be long this time…
I might not see the next sunrise.
Yet my embers will continue to shine
like the eyes of a newborn baby…

1/17/1975

Capturing an Evening
on the Beach!

When we're together, the sea
transforms into a silver mirror
with fairytale reflections...
Rocks become hills of ivory and gold,
crabs appear like rubies
spread across the beach...
Fish dance over ocean waves
and seahorses fly in the wind
with legendary speed...

***

...Our hands interlock,
pulsating like two naked hearts...
The radiant moon dims the silverware
displayed for sale on the beach sidewalk...

***

You embrace me
despite the glares of passersby...
I listen to your heart,
the beating of the wind and thunder...

***

*Ya Habibi,** my darling...
When you leave my sight,

---

* *Habibi* is a term that is commonly used in Arabic to mean "my darling" or "my
  love." When *Ya* is added, it indicates that the speaker is calling to someone, in this
  case, the beloved.

my eyes become scars of a half-healed wound...

***

Friend of the ocean...one night
my body transformed into a record
carrying your voice, your handprints...
I'm spinning on top of the darkness,
above the silence...the needle
of memory runs on top of me,
and I hear your every word,
feel your every touch...
I love you!...

Ocean's Hotel—Night's Beach—
6/30/1976

Two years later: *The moment you lifted me up on that same beach two years later, I touched the sky and felt the wind's spirit. The night enveloped me like the open arms of a nurturing mother. The stars were glowing deeply bright....I felt like a new star being drawn on the maps of astrologers, a star sought by lovers....It was the same beach...the same time...the same magic. I was no longer certain that you were the same man...but what difference does that make? The feelings were the same...even more intense, more delicate, and refined. They were sculpted by an indifference to perfection and detail...focused on the moment's essence...*

Capturing R.F. *

Before you get bored and leave,
teach me how to turn my right cheek
to those who've just devoured my left cheek...
Teach me how to pray out loud
for those who've cut out my tongue...
Teach me how to tear away the radar of knowing
that stretches like a spider web across my soul.
Teach me how to give freely
to those criminals who auction me off...
Teach me how to love my friends when I know
I'm capable of loving my enemies!...

9/3/1977

---

* R.F. are the initials of a friend that Samman refers to earlier in the poem "Capturing a Gun!"

A Fleeting Moment Captures Me

Like a pearl, I opened my oyster shell for you,
but you turned it into an ashtray
and left!...

***

I knocked at night's door
to see your familiar face,
but one of your many masks greeted me
growling.

***

The night was never ending like my wound.
I'm alone, cold, and poor
like the holes in a beggar's sock
on a winter's eve...
Darkness falls and I collapse
like an avalanche of muddied snow...
Here I fell...here the grass grew...
here my wounds scabbed...
When Dawn arrived, he thought I was a flower
burnt by a thunderbolt.
So, he covered me with dew...

***

I'm devastated not because you left me,
but because I'm grieving who I thought you were...
Ah, how did you manage to wear a lover's mask so long!
I loved you in front of three seas:
the Red, the White, and the Atlantic...

I married my spirit with yours in front of three gods:
tenderness, affection, and hope...
It's difficult to stay alive
when everything around me is dead:
the doors, the windows, the horizon,
the rain, the plow, the trees,
and the person I loved,
loved... loved ...

***

When will the sharp sword of my will
come inside the forest of my love
that is so wild, unyielding, uncontrollable?
(Memories of our fleeting moments capture me.)
When will the sharp sword of my will
cut a window for the sun
and a door for my escape?...

11/2/1977

Capturing an Argument

Our words are more evasive than
fish eluding their predators.

***

I become silent as dust,
as fragmented as sand...
My silence was a cry for help that you didn't hear!
Our love is now a dagger—
we take turns stabbing each other...
we glare at each other like two hungry dogs
barking in the snow!...

***

I have an uncontrollable urge to beat you up,
but I throw a crumbled tissue at you instead...
You say I'm made of steel,
I feel fragile as ashes but, at the same time,
vicious as a scythe's blade...

***

A volcano erupts in my heart,
so—calmly and silently—I chew on ice
without drinking from my cup...
Horrified, I realize—when seeds of discord grow,
they turn into electric fences called "breakup."

9/6/1975

Capturing Telepathy

I can't stop thinking about you…
I remember you,
I dwell in the intensity of your presence…
At the same time, I put a lot of effort
into finishing my engrossing book…
Yet something ethereal happens,
my innermost secret keys become captive
to a mysterious magnetism that attracts them…

And here am I thinking of you intensely,
I remember you,
I dwell in the intensity of your presence,
I hear your voice
and I'm certain that you're suffering like me
in exactly the same way and at exactly the same moment…
We are… at this very second…communicating
across some spiritual telephone line,
each of us being drawn toward the other—in some way—
through ethereal lines in a mysterious universe.

***

Please, stop shouting in my ear like that
when you're so far away…

8/5/1976

Capturing the Parachute of a Dream

You go to buy bread and come back without your teeth…
You go to find water and return with your intestines hanging out…
You go to buy apples and return with an apple,
but leave your woman torn to pieces at the gate of a hospital
collapsing under a rain of fire...

Roosters now crow at sunset,
cats in heat yowl in mid-August instead of February,
ants abandon dry fountains,
mice wander over dead electric wires…
Eating is self-indulgence,
bathing an ambition.

***

You leave your room and go to the beach
to remember breathing is free,
but return with a bullet in your lung…

***

All earth's elements are disturbed—
life inhabits death.
If it weren't for you…
if it weren't for my passionate dream of you,
if I weren't sure you will be reborn

as a youth full of untamed desires,
I would've collapsed on the beach,
empty as a bullet
that's missed its target...

Beirut-7/5/1976
This poem has been translated into Farsi.

Capturing a Question Mark!

O stranger,
where do songs go
after we hear them?

***

Where do words of love go
after we say them?

***

Where do precious moments go
after we live them?

***

Where do candle flames go
after they burn?

***

Where do embraces go
after we part?

***

Where does thunder vanish after it roars?
What happens to forest storms after they move on?
What about embers after they burn?
Tell me, my love, so I can wait for you there.

7/21/1976
This poem has been translated into English

Capturing Beginnings
of a Breakup

The song coming from the window torments us...
I remember when we first heard it a year ago
before our love died and left us with ashes
and rain: the mud of indifference...

***

These photographs torment us...
Do you see the passion in our eyes,
our joyful laughter?
Look at our faces now,
portraits of apathy and indifference, somewhat depressed,
pale as an old ragged dress...

***

The time we spend together torments us...
The room that used to shelter us like twins,
feels like a stone womb,
a prison with thousands of walls, doors, and locks
set between us...
Do you see how silence has become our master,
estrangement our jailer?
Do you see how polite caution, hostile in intent,
pollutes our conversation?...

***

These candles torment us...

Their flames no longer light a single spark in our eyes,
or send a fiery current through our veins...

***

This incense torments us...
Its scent has become one of depression and lethargy,
the yawning of priests in an abandoned temple...

***

Nothing in this universe can encounter anything else
without a reaction, without a smell or taste,
except our time together...
I hold my ear to a glass of water, the ice crackles
as though it were boiling.
Our inert meetings don't boil or freeze,
have no hot or cold, only the silence of death.
Do you realize ice cubes have more life than
our music,
our candles,
our pictures,
our moments together?
Even ice cubes yell:
The time of love has ended...
The time of parting has come!...
So...who will tell the other first?

***

Whoever loved the other more
will be the first to leave...
Whoever remembers the passionate past
will reject the apathy of now...
Which one of us will say the word "breakup" first?

78

Which one of us will first admit:
nothing of our love remains
in the mirror of memory
except what's left inside the mirror
after the memory is gone...

2/5/1976

Capturing a Lost Kiss

The border patrol officers stopped me
as I was coming from seeing you, my love
(as I was going to see you, my love).
They searched my pockets and found stars.
They said, *Arrest her for possessing explosives*!

***

They asked me, *O mysterious woman,*
what are you doing on the streets at night?
I'm trying to capture a lost kiss
that escaped into the past—the moment
he kissed me by the door of Neptune's Rome, the shelter.
Nearby, people were fleeing from bombs…
the sky was a sheet of red…
the streets were exploding gunpowder...
Time was a fleeting moment…
life, a cat vanishing around a corner…that is invisible…
But the lost kiss infused me with passionate life—
even among all the dead....The officers said,
We'll arrest her for acts of terrorism as well…

***

The officers said, *Inspection!*
Open your trunk, open your eyes wide.
We want to search them!
They searched my eyes and saw your face
at the moment I was giving you a rose
and you said, "I'm hungry" and devoured the rose!!

***

I escaped their gunshots,
seeking refuge in our familiar coffee shop,
its aromas, its desserts, and hot tea…
I ran back towards that untamed yet tender moment
when you were devouring my rose
and when we laughed as if we were crying.
That moment—suspended in time—
had spent months running away
on time's train without its fire lessening!…
The warmth of your kiss never left me!…

***

They asked me, *What will you do if we let you go?*
I told them, "I'll continue to chase that lost kiss
and I will continue to plant jasmines
in his dimples when he smiles!"
They asked, *Do you have any weapons?*
So, I showed them your picture.
They asked, *What are all these papers?*
"Love letters," I responded.

This is when their commander yelled,
Publications! Publications that solicit life!
Kill her! Love? Kill her now!

***

When their bullets went through my head,
I didn't feel much pain, for at that moment,
I was in your arms on the sidewalk of Neptune's Shelter,
your tender kiss enveloping me.
I finally managed to capture it!…

12/31/1977

Capturing a Fairy Tale

…He's bewitchingly handsome…
"Handsome" doesn't do him justice.
His face radiates longing for the unknown,
his forehead, a hunger for the impossible,
his cheeks are shadowed with sadness—godly and mysterious—
his eyes ignite with volcanoes of desire,
his lips glow with lavas of madness.

***

…He's enchanting beyond words,
impossible to capture in art, words,
music…or even magic acts…
If Michelangelo had seen him,
he would've decorated the hills of Florence
with this man's statues…Rafael, seeing him,
would have reworked his paintings of Christ.

***

…He's charming, a fairytale hero
whose presence turns ultimate darkness into light,
transforms sunshine into a brilliant midnight…
When he touches my face, I drift into oblivion…
I fall and fall and fall,
tumbling over the mountains of his chest and shoulders,
his silence and mysteries…
…I vanish into unearthly bliss...

8/1/1976

Capturing a Pierced Memory

I'm beginning to forget everything,
but you...I'm beginning to forget the eyes, the lips
of lovers whom I imagined were torches,
lighting my uneven and rocky path...

***

I'm beginning to forget...
...was his mole on the right or left cheek?
I do remember stumbling over it every time we kissed...
That man made me miserable...and I made him miserable too.
I'm beginning to forget...
...was the scar on his right or left arm?
I remember how he tried drowning me
in a pool of anesthesia...and failed.
Yet, I loved him...

***

My memories are starting to fade
as your body becomes the night,
your lips the horizon...
With you, all of the past I thought would be painful
—when it shrivels into mere memory—
now slides off my skin...like dust from the street...

***

I can now listen
to the music I enjoyed with lovers long ago...
and dream of no one but you.
With you, that music no longer wounds my heart...

83

You managed to pierce those memories
and empty out the dust
of my past loves.

***

I'm truly beginning to drown
in the pool of your beard,
drift into the forests of your mustache…
I'm beginning…to love you…
I've kept you close under my skin…many times…
But beware of my pierced memory—
You too may fall right out of it…
one day!…

9/2/1976

Capturing a Moment
of Vulnerability

How beautiful it is to be with you…
Ordinary conversations become exciting
like Einstein's theory,
toxins turn into purple clouds I fly upon.
There's not a single nail that can hurt my body…

***

How beautiful it is to be with you…
There's no yesterday, no tomorrow…
the boat of the moment takes us
to islands we imagine
no one has set foot upon…
to mountains where no human lung
has ever breathed the air…

***

How beautiful it is to be with you…
Waves of repressed joy overtake me
mysteriously and suddenly,
I become vulnerable to your glances,
your silence, your words.
I love you… I love you… I love you…

Morning in Tripoli~4/13/1975

Capturing Punishment

This is punishment:
For you to have your own two legs,
a different night in a different bed,
a different dream, a different fate,
other friends,
another path.
And I love you!...

***

This is punishment:
For you to walk away,
an independent person...
who thinks about people I don't know,
remembers things we didn't experience together,
who listens to voices I never heard,
shakes hands I never touched.
And I love you!...

***

This is punishment:
That they have cut you from my rib,
gave you another body, different from mine,
a different memory, different interests,
and a different life.
And I still love you after all that!...

10/22/1977

Capturing a Lusty Moment

Ah, when you move
every part of your body greets the other,
expressing gladness to be next to it!

***

Ferocious and desirable…
everything about you is ferocious and desirable.
When you stand up
with your shameless stature,
my lust becomes a dragonfly chasing you
among shimmering fields.
Like a shark, my teeth sink into you.

***

You are a festival of masculinity
to freshmen girls…
who dream about you,
who get pregnant as they
make chaste love to you.

***

Ferocious and desirable…
every time you leave me,
even if it's to a nearby tree,
I feel the emptiness of a woman who miscarried
after her lover has been murdered…

***

Ferocious and desirable…
I gaze at you
and wonder how I can cocoon you here...

12/18/1976

Capturing a Flying Beak!

Don't wear that poor
feathered hat,
a carnival *tarboosh.**

***

Don't drag me on streets
crowded with drunken fools…
Don't drown me with balloons
and kisses like holiday fireworks.
Don't toot that blowout whistle,
that flying beak…

***

Don't tell me, "Happy New Year!"
I'm *not* happy when you're a lost child
blinded by fake decorations…
Don't scar your face with false joy.
Spit out that blowout whistle,
the beak of ignorant birds…

***

---

* *Tarboosh* or *tarbush,* more recognized as *fez* in the West, is a red, brimless, flat-topped, and cylindrical hat worn by men in eastern Mediterranean countries (Webster). It's made of velvet or red felt and typically includes a silk tassel that hangs down its side. Widely accepted in the Middle East, it was popularized during the Ottoman era. It is still respected as a traditional/conservative form of male dress, but it has also come, in some contexts, to be regarded as mere costume or an ethnic cliché. Samman is using the word here to criticize the lover's assumption of a false and clichéd masculine identity that distracts him from seeing social and political oppression.

Every year, you remain the same… my darling…
a bird who's lost his real beak…

***

Don't you see the vampires
behind the Christmas lights
shutting us in from every side?
Don't you see they invent carnival joys
to distract us from pounding nails
into their gallows' wood!…

New Year's Eve-1977-1978

Capturing the Murderer
and the Murdered!

...Here I am again
with two men—
The one I used to love,
and the one I now hate.
Both are you!...

***

A wall has been built
between us three.
In vain, I try to destroy it,
using my glass axe of fake optimism...

***

Ah, what do I tell (you both)?
My heart—a colorful wave—
surrenders its boat to the winds of passion.
Ah, what can I tell (you both)?
I forgot that love is magic dust,
glowing on the beach of time.
Childlike, I try to capture it
...it slips through my fingers
if I cling too tightly...

***

...Here I am again, as usual,
with two men—
One man let me down,
I let down the other...

91

You are both...
The man who killed me
and the man I killed.
You are both...
The man I loved
and the man I hate.
You are both!...

***

...Here I am again,
alone and isolated,
a forest bleeding across the horizon...
In vain, I build my house
with an ant's patience.
In vain, I gather my fragments
(scattered between both of you)...

***

...Here I am again
with two men —
One I used to love,
one I now hate.
Both are you...

***

I float in our love's ruins...
Time's watchdog barks,
chases me, and bites off the edges of my memory.
(Steel nightingales shriek as fire melts their larynxes.)
Happiness turns away...

Caught by the fishhook of longing,
my body dangles in abandoned forests,
like a person hung on the tree of dawn.

***

I see you in a vision,
so death commits suicide!...

***

The green stars of forgetfulness
rush to grow in my burning earth...
I strip you away from my body
like a snake shedding its skin.
I strip you away
as the wounded unshroud at sunset
to wear tomorrow's sun.

***

Farewell to fearing the charm of one
and dreading the other's ferocity...
Farewell to the magic of one
and the other's deadly touch!

***

Farewell to the warmth of spring days,
followed by the violence of winter's frost.
Farewell to warring climates,
silent aggression followed by lethal cries.
Farewell to you both: the murdered and the murderer...

12/1/1977

Capturing the Arriving Man

Come close or stay away,
fill my days with swan-white memories
and the songs of fountains,
with the laughter of wheat swaying in the wind,
with the vibrancy of forest light…
Or leave me and return on another cold night,
whipped and bleeding with rain…

***

Come close or stay away,
fill me with the tenderness of winter kisses,
stolen by the cart of the chestnut seller…
Or leave me, a lonely prey…next to the window
of some house, half-lit and locked.
Come and let light-filled peace
enfold me like a child asleep…
Or abandon me
and let bitter longing grow over my tongue…
It makes no difference,
for I love you
just like I loved the ones before you
and just like I will love the ones after you…

***

It's all the same to me,
whether you're caring or cruel…
—sunny day or stormy night—
because the geysers deep inside of me
explode in all climates,

94

all time zones, seasons, continents,
washing everything with love…love…

***

I am a woman who does not cry
because she knows no season
but the season of love…
Now, I truly love you,
just as I loved the ones before you…truly…
and as I'll love the man who comes after you!…

11/12/1977

Capturing the Cries of Screams without Mouths

If you love me, you're my only enemy!

***

If you're with me, then you're against me!

***

Do you love me?
Do you know how to sew up a hole in the heart?
Do you know how to stitch shut the tubes of sadness
that bleed from my soul?
And how to put muzzles on screams without mouths?
Can you stop a soul from dying?

***

If you love me, you're my only enemy...
Every small betrayal you (secretly) enact
is (a rehearsal for) life's big betrayal.
Every small lie is a small death
that reminds me of life's big lie
that we swallow (uselessly) every night
along with our sedatives and sleeping pills.
Every mistake you make is a crime
against joy because it shows me
how fragile and fake it is.

***

If you love me, you're my only enemy…
Pain has vaccinated me against your words,
sleek as a snake's tongue…
I've become immune to your dangerous love.
I am a woman armored with bruises…
Before love, I mastered the art of pain.
I know that thing that shines in your hand
is the dagger's blade,
not the crescent of loyalty…
I see clearly
because, with you, my eyes are shut!…

***

If you love me, you're my only enemy…
When I indulge your caresses,
I feel like someone sentenced to death.
I smile at the electric chair,
flirt with the suicide's noose,
dance with my master of whips.

4/12/1977

Capturing My Scattered Remains

When the fever was overtaking me,
one organ after another,
one bone after another...
I thought of all my loved ones,
one after another,
one after another,
their suspicious words,
their false longing to see me,
the lies they told me,
the lies I told them,
all our honesty...
And while the fever was overtaking me,
from artery to artery,
I wondered where they were...

***

My remains are scattered on the bed...
my severed head rests near the pillow...
a hand is by the nightstand...
a foot is on the other side of the bed,
where cockroaches are crawling around it...
I see clearly now:
No one was ever hard on me...
I truly want things to stay the same.
I want to remain alone with my music,
my madness, my pens, my grief, my dreams.
My unplugged phone is a witness to that...
I hide—quick—like a bead of mercury...hide!...

***

Alone, I discovered myself,
a stealthy child who escaped her school bus.
I was alone with them,
I am alone without them and...
I am forever alone *because* of them!...

The Night of-3/17/1977

99

Capturing a Moment's Longing

If only the phone would ring right now,
I'd answer...anyone...*Ya Habibi.**
I'm alone tonight, trembling,
inhabited with longing...I'm alone.
Life is not long enough for all my difficult choices.
I'm alone...
Love floods me...
To any human who whispers right now, "Good evening,"
I would reply, *Ya Habibi.*...What a perfect evening for love....

***

I *am* love,
I long to give!...
The other side called "the beloved" is a mere myth
that I cover over with a cloak of love
I have carefully woven...I...I...I...

***

Love, for me, is a matter of timing.
There is no preference for one man over another,
except in timing!...

***

I'm still waiting for a voice I don't know,
someone to love instantly!...

---

* *Ya Habibi* is a term that is commonly used in Arabic to mean "my love" or "my beloved." Samman uses the word in its masculine form, the feminine being *Ya Habibti*. The word is not limited to couples or people in love, but can also be used as a term of endearment among close friends and relatives. Here, Samman uses the term to emphasize the narrator's loneliness and desperation for connection.

Love, permeating deep inside, floods me, overflows
like electricity shaken from a frantic storm.

***

I'm still waiting for a man I don't know,
so I may love him tonight...
I don't ask that he be handsome,
rich, smart, or a genius...
It's enough for him to be silent,
so I may write over his silence
the million words I long to hear...
I want him to be alone,
so I can imagine he's been waiting for me,
I want him to be sad,
so I can imagine he's like me.
Then, after that, I will love him
and tyrannize him with my love...

7/6/1976

Capturing a Book's Dedication

Sometimes the heart bleeds
more than custom allows,
so we run to formal rhetoric
like that found in book dedications!...

I wonder which you would prefer:
My dirty naked wound,
running with the blood of confused chaos
or my mask of propriety?...

11/16/1975

Capturing a Fleeting Melody

It's that old melody
we listened to together
—I don't remember if I liked it or not—
But I know we heard it together...and it heard us...
...It recorded our voices
and captured, inside of it,
those fragile moments,
fleeting and luminous...
And here it is playing them over again...

***

It's that old melody again...
I remember it was raining that night.
Where is the sound of the wind?
Why doesn't the storm suddenly erupt
out of the heart's fake warmth
and illusionary spring?

***

Why doesn't my heart stop
to shamelessly scream like a child
the name of that lost love,
to write it on the walls of night like a banner
(for distribution to lovers in brochures),
and to hammer it on the trees
like an old verdict of execution?

***

Ah, let my heart scream
the name of that lost love,
as it struggles in the confusion
of that love's illusion and reality,
like a face staring into ten mirrors,
looking for itself…

***

It's that old melody again,
but without the storm…
Ah, why doesn't it rain tonight
like it rained that night—
so my heart can imagine it's still alive?
Ah, a flicker of lightning
to rip my heart open like a sword,
so blood can flow in it once more!...

5/22/1976

Capturing Birds That Morph into Monkeys

...I will not let them
steal my green blood
or my limitless capacity for joy, love, life, and...flight...

***

...I will not let them
steal my wings...
They will not turn me into a species
incapable of flying,
proficient in hatred,
a species whose habitat is underground sewage systems...

***

I'm a thunderbird,
free as thunder, honest as thunder, public as thunder.
No surveillance tower can steal the word "love"
that I utter for you and for this universe.
I refuse to let their surveillance steal from my eyes a single spark
of love, wonder, and curiosity.
...I will not let them clip my wings...
and deform my soul,
imprint it with badges of blind hatred.
And I will continue to cry for anyone's clipped wings...
for we humans are born flying
(though some may choose to morph into monkeys)...

***

They can gossip with tongues
like hell's poisoned spears,
they can stone me with angry glares—sharp as lasers,
they can confront me with silence,
but I will continue to be free—alive!
I will continue to be love, freedom, and honesty...
I will be a bird that flies beyond boundaries,
away from lifeboats, over iron fences,
through windows with embroidered curtains.
I will be a tigress,
running amid trees of freedom,
soaring over bountiful forests,
chasing your shadow...
I love you, I love them, I love you!...

8/22/1977

Capturing the Word "Masculinity"

At the moment of our parting,
you hid your hand in your pockets
as if to escape holding mine...
Ah, this is separation...

***

All of that stern rejection
that my body confronted you with
was not the determination of our grandfathers...
It was the will of my own soul—
which you didn't believe lived in me.
It's been difficult for you to believe
that a woman has a soul and a will,
not just a body!...

***

The memory of your pain consumes me,
just as my own pain consumes me,
the pain you never believed I could feel
(perhaps because the word "pain" is masculine!!)

***

"Pain." "Giving." "Loyalty." "Sincerity."
All are masculine words in school books:
With you, I strove for a language
beyond graduation!...

9/9/1977

Capturing Nostalgia

What kind of love are we hanging onto
when, at the end, the electric chair
only fits one person?
—Goodbye and don't bother to ask who's guilty—
You said goodbye, went inside an orange, and locked its skin.
I said goodbye…and entered into a ball of night,
and here it is rolling over bumpy ladders of forgetfulness…

***

The windows of nostalgia open up,
the winds blow me out again…and again…
I'm a yellow leaf,
lost in a hurricane…

9/17/1976

Capturing a Gasp

When you ignited me
like a lighthouse in Eden
overlooking three continents,
I didn't mean to summon the flies!...

                        ***

So, how can you imagine I'm cheating on you?

                                        1/3/1975

109

Capturing Another Orbit

Stop breathing over my papers!
Move your body away from my room's ceiling,
spare me your blind love
that won't bend for anything...
For I'm purely myself...purely...
I laugh purely...I cry purely...

***

You come to me with your love,
your madness, your storms
after it's too late...

***

Now,
I'm on the beach,
on the other side of the river...
I see you,
I hear you,
but our paths will never meet again...never...

***

Ah, is it too late?
I'm the queen of madness, freedom, challenge,
and love...love...
Is there anything that can quench my desires?
Why does silent disappointment
stifle my spontaneous cries?...
Ah, night...
night after night...

Ah, wound…
wound after wound…
Ah, disgust, bewildering disgust,
heart sorrow, dream sorrow,
the sorrow of memory…
vertigo, vertigo...
May this be the end of attempted escapes,
even from earth's gravity and society's circle.
But...
But…light has another path,
the solution is outside the orbit of the game!...

10/19/1977

Capturing Contradiction

Ah, how I hate to love you,
to be inhabited every moment
by that mysterious pain,
the longing—unending—
to hear your voice...

***

Ah, how I hate *not* to love you,
my days foggy and pale like pages
of an old, dusty (forgotten) book.

***

Ah, how I hate to love you,
to become a white filly
that runs in the forest of curiosity,
rejecting any muzzle or restraint...

***

Ah, how I hate *not* to love you,
to become a wolf
that eats or is eaten by its pack...
instead of remaining a white dove
that trembles in your hands,
a naked heart pulsating with life.

***

Ah, how I hate to love you...
You pierce through me like a spear,

roam freely inside me
like a ghost trapped in a haunted house.

***

Ah, how I hate *not* to love you...
How can I not love you...
when you contain stones, forests,
winds, cactus flowers, storms,
wild roses, springs, minerals,
elements...and the dream,
all that is infinite and glorious
in our fragile existence...

7/25/1976

Capturing 13 Owls

3 sevens,
long nails,
13 owls
fly away when you arrive...
I love you and that's a good omen!...

***

I love the way you truly are,
not their legends of you...
I love your secret anger,
not the way you smile
into the lenses of photographers...
I love your black thorns,
the nights of terror when you hide
from their chains of humiliation.

***

3 sevens,
long nails,
13 owls,
thunderbolts and night
follow you...
I love you and that's the *only* good omen!...

9/12/1977

Capturing an Eye Resisting a Chisel... (The Eye Always Resists the Chisel...)

I travel,
my suitcase is forgetfulness.
My passport states:
Citizen of The Kingdom of Indifference.
I have a vaccination certificate for:
chicken pox, cholera...and one more
against your deadly love...

***

Before I left,
I said loudly, "I love you!"
That meant, *I was done with you!*...

***

Gossip is love's exile...
Before, my love was a whisper,
my voice was silence,
but you didn't hear me...

***

One day,
your love wounded me
like a paper cut—
painful, sharp...a little blood,
silent, secretive,
and familiar to those who have experienced

sharp cuts, the eyes staring back
white with innocence...

***

One day,
your love cut me deeply.
And I loved you deeply...
You turned me into a frost princess
inside your snow castle.
I'm the wild child of nature...
I belong to freedom's forests,
and you were demanding from me
some romantic story
with its rhetorical professions of love.
You were incapable of understanding
that honesty dwells in silence.
That day, I looked at you...
I was an eye resisting a chisel...
the eye always resists the chisel!...

***

Now, I close my eyes
and examine your face,
its pale sweetness,
your smile of forgetful tenderness,
your nimble fingers
like those of con artists and pickpockets.
I loved you once in silence,
I suffered in silence...

***

I no longer love you...
My heart no longer lives and dies,

116

waiting for your phone calls.
You can no longer bury my treasure
…in a grave…
I'm no longer a turtle that can only live
…inside your shell…
You can no longer control my soul
like a stubborn demon from hell.
I now see your body
as a vast desert of cracked salt…

***

Your love was…and no longer is.
Your love is a past tense
without a verb…it has no function…
I no longer love you…no…no…
The "no" I scream is not a "no" that negates,
but a "no" that effaces you completely
from my life…

***

The day I declared, "I love you,"
I meant, *I'm leaving you*!...
Now, you'll be glad to see me,
but you won't know what you've lost.
You won't be able to tell the difference between
what I give you today and what I gave you yesterday.
You never knew what you had,
and you never knew how to value it…
Now, you'll enjoy death with me
after you've failed life with me…

***

Now, our meetings will be comfortable,
amusing like some absurd joke,
without fever or tension,
without bitter love...
Now, when you take me to your forest,
only I will know the kind of Arabian filly
I could've been—drenched in passion,
tender, and loyal.
Any warm body I give to you, any forest...
this is your only choice,
so you better take it.
And I caution you never to say:
you were, we were, I was...

***

You were the chisel,
I was the eye that resisted it
and didn't break.
The eye always resists the chisel!...

12/22/1977

Capturing a Moment of Health

As I tumble in the luxury
of health, life, love, and music,
I am fully aware of the Death Master
hiding beneath my bed...
I hear Him breathing,
a clock ticking!...

***

Come closer, Death Master,
I'm your woman...and this is your bed.
May your wish be my wish:
May my light,
—the moment it extinguishes in my eyes—
brighten another being.

***

Death Master,
I'm your loyal bride
—men are mere waiting rooms—
So come,
let our love blossom and multiply.
Let our wedding
be of use to the guests
in Hotel Mother Earth...
and let my death enrich
one of our guests—
that's all the dowry I ask!...

12/15/1977

Capturing an Explosion

I write…
I know nothing else,
I hate nothing else,
I love nothing else!…

***

I love wearing nice clothes,
the company of shallow, rich men,
their fancy yachts and private planes.

***

But writing is my personal madness,
my loyal obsession…
it steers me away from all that.
I eat my loaf of bread with that wanderer
who sits beneath official statues about to explode…
I float, a drop in the river of blood,
across impoverished alleys and muddy stones.
(I just heard an explosion that broke the window, but I keep writing.)
Writing is my explosion…
the shattered glass is the asphalt of my path,
my bread's dough since I can remember…
The affinity between me and explosions
is a forgotten truth worthy of recording…

***

My life is a series of explosions
in the cities I choose,
the streets I know,

in my windows, my arteries, my soul.
Explosions are my lifetime, my destiny.
I am the daughter of this exploding dirt
and these explosive times...

***

So stranger, why does your sudden explosion
into my life surprise me?

10/29/1977

Capturing Fear
(In a Rose Garden
Sanitized with Alcohol)

We walked in a garden,
ideal in its cleanliness and order,
like a hospital for the wealthy...
The flowers were sanitized cotton,
infused with vitamins.
I took off my coat,
threw it to you as I ran and jumped!
Coldheartedly, you caught it
and hung it on the branches of propriety,
as you looked over your shoulders with embarrassment!

                                                ***

The medicinal smell of alcohol emanated from the flowers,
—the garden had turned into an oxygen tank—
...I couldn't breathe the air.
European tourists, cold, polished, indifferent,
seemed like the rest of the statues in the garden.
I imagined spending the rest of my life with you,
turning into one of these statues.
A desperate need overcame me
to chant every Arabic curse I knew.
I wanted to throw myself onto the chest
of the first Arab man I meet who truly loves the desert,
truly lives it...instead of flirting with it

and then running away.
I saw my future with you:
We grow old together, glued to the grasses of a Geneva garden:
…Swamps…Swamps…Swamps…

Geneva~4/10/1976

Capturing Disappointment Disguised as Wisdom

...Love is a magical white unicorn.
Whoever falls under its spell
will be torn apart, tossed
into a muddy pit,
and cry for a long time,
waiting for wounds to heal.
If you straddle and ride love,
it'll take you to fantasylands.
What's important is that you *ride love*,
not let it ride you...

***

Don't remove your mask
in love's alley,
keep it on your face—firmly—
cover your wounds and the secrets of your soul.
Remember, every slip of a mask
leads to a severe stab in the heart...

***

Love is as we imagine it to be,
invented only...for dreaming...
Anyone who loves sincerely will get torn apart
just like any dreamer
who insists on continuing the dream,
even after waking!...

2/5/1976

Capturing a Window

I'm no longer alone...
you can no longer destroy me...
This foolish and childish heart of mine
once pulsated for nothing except your vanity.
Now, it beats for a vaster and far nobler body,
the source of roses and wheat, joy and prosperity...
Its seasons never lie...

***

I'm no longer alone and isolated...
you can no longer destroy me...
For the one I love has existed before you and me
and will remain after you and me,
capable of loving everyone.
So, I am no longer alone and isolated
I am no longer alone and isolated.
...Here I am mending on an island
where hard-working people like me labor
for a heart as if it were a loaf of bread
and for a loaf of bread as if it were a warm heart.
Farewell to imprisonment inside your body,
itself locked up inside a fortress of privilege.
If you had ever starved (like me) on a night of war,
you too would've found the window!...

4/17/1976

Capturing a Corpse
beneath the Lines

With my own two hands,
I opened your prison door,
walked in,
locked the door, and secured it with a latch.
I wrapped chains around my body
and bribed the prison guard...to not let me escape.
I declared my love for you...

**

I let your will overpower mine...
I imprisoned the sun far away,
I rejected it
if it didn't pierce
through your cloak...

**

The rain... the awe... the wonderment,
my longing to run wild
in the streets of unknown cities,
I tied them all up in ropes
and flagellated them...

**

I nailed down my dreams
—free and transparent like the wings of a butterfly—
and used them to adorn my prison walls.
I declared I love you!
But I died.

You can find my corpse lying beneath the lines
on this page…
Lift the words from this page
like you would sweep snow from a marble gravestone.
You will find me lying there,
a suffocated bird.

Zürich~5/26/1976

Capturing a Moment of Pain

Wake up you foolish, sad woman,
sleeping in the cocoon of fever,
come out into the sun,
abandon to darkness the rot of memories...
and the rot of dreams...

***

Wake up you foolish, sad woman,
get out of the dragon's mouth,
run naked in the forest of rain,
let its raindrops wake your sleeping pores,
your body fallen into the anesthesia of depression...

***

Wake up you foolish, sad woman,
devour the men at the table,
eat their caviar,
drink their turtle soup,
sail off in their ivory yachts,
and discover the beauty of silver and gold,
the glow of diamonds.
Stop searching
for eyes
that have the sparkle of honesty and passion,
and sincerity solid as gold.

***

Wake up you foolish, sad woman,
whose face looks at me in the mirror

every time I come into the bathroom
and vomit my heart's blood.
This moment is the only truth.
Remember that.
Lying is the only human truth.
Remember that.
Forgetting is the only medicine.
Remember that...

12/17/1977

Capturing a Small Earthquake

What's happening to me?
Frozen are the tears of my heart,
frozen is the blood in my eyes.
My grief has transformed into an ice mountain...

***

My wound is too deep for me to confront,
too bloody for me to dare remove the bandages—
the bridge inside of me between my wild secret world
and my tame exterior world has collapsed.
There was no refuge for me except to confess
—to myself at least—
that I live on the wilder side of the bank.
I dream of an island with an electric fence,
an ocean, a sky, stars, cats, swallows,
and all the plants and animals,
except those that are more harmful than dinosaurs:
those naked monkeys called *homo sapiens*.

***

I want to be alone with my heartbeat,
so I can hear the sound of time.
I want to be alone with my brain waves,
so I can hear one of the voices of truth.
I want to climb the tree of knowledge
and be nourished by nothing but it.
All of these landslides in the sands of my soul
are cries of deprivation begging to drink more
from the fountain of caustic awareness...

The night of-3/17/1977

Capturing a Moment
of Humiliation

Let the heart be proud of a moment's confession: I love you.
I love you. I love you. I love you.
I know you for who you are,
and I still love you.

***

My only oasis is your drought,
my only safety is your betrayal,
my only harbor is your departure,
my only happiness is your infidelity,
my wounds' only peace is your dagger.

***

I love you as you are,
I miss you as you are,
I accept you as you are…

***

So let the heart be proud of a moment's confession: Come back.
I still love you,
I hate everything about you…
And I still love you!

***

The day we parted…
I stood in front of the mirror…
I saw no reflection,

not a trace of me.
I stood on the pharmacy scale,
the pointer remained at zero.
I stood in line to get a cinema ticket,
but the clerk did not see me
and sold the ticket to the person behind me...

***

You shut me in the flower of your fierce love,
planted your thorns in my soul
and completely absorbed me...

***

So let the heart be proud of a moment's humiliation: Come back.
I hate everything about you...
I love you. I love you. I love you.

Now, yesterday, and tomorrow

GHADA SAMMAN

A BIOGRAPHICAL SKETCH

Ghada Samman is one of the most prolific and influential Arab women writers of the twentieth and twenty-first centuries. She is a highly respected voice for human rights and feminism in the Arab world, speaking up against the atrocities of war and social injustice. Samman was born in Damascus, Syria, in 1942 and spent a good portion of her early life there. She has been residing in France since 1985 while continuing to maintain a home in Beirut, Lebanon. After her mother, Salma Ruwaiha, died at the age of thirty when Samman was only five, she was raised by her grandmother, Khayriah, and her father, Dr. Ahmad Samman, professor and dean of the faculty of law at the University of Damascus and then Syria's minister of education. He played a critical role in shaping her love for Arabic and Western literature and instilled in her a passion for music, art, and nature. She credits her father for her resilient spirit, strong will, and self-determination (El-Hage 137). Samman learned French in her early years from her mother, a writer who used a pen name due to strict cultural norms governing women. Samman attended both French and Arabic-curriculum-based schools and considers French her first language, Arabic her second, and English her third (El-Hage 137).

Early on, Samman's rebellious spirit came through in her writing as she challenged rigid social and religious norms that are imprinted in women's psyche. In November 1961, when she was 19, *Jaridat al-Nasr al-Suriyah* (*Al-Nasr Syrian Newspaper*) published her essay "Our Constitution—We the Liberated Women," also known as "Let us Pray for the Slave who is Flogged." This essay was written in response to some women in Hamma, Syria, who refused to exercise their right to vote (Wayne 572). Samman proclaimed, "...let us pray for the butterflies who refuse to break out of their cocoons and to confront the storm. They have become used to being jailed worms" (qtd. In DeLamotte, Meeker, and OBarr 86). Here, Samman expresses, perhaps in a somewhat ironic tone, that women, especially in repressive societies, must struggle to confront and break free of the social and religious mores that deny them personal freedom.

Samman received her BA in English literature from the Faculty of Arts at Damascus University in 1963 and traveled to Beirut in 1964 to get her MA in literature from the American University of Beirut (AUB). There, she did her thesis, "The Theater of the Absurd," and in 1965, published her second short-story collection, *La Bahr Fi Bayrut* (*There Is No Sea in Beirut*), followed by *Layal al-Ghuraba* (*Nostalgia Nights*) in 1966. In 1973, she published her first poetry collection, *Love*, followed by her first novel, *Beirut 75* (1974) in which she predicted the start of the Lebanese Civil War in 1975. Samman chose to remain in Beirut until 1985 and wrote novels and poetry that describe war-torn Lebanon. *Beirut Nightmares* (1977), a novel written in diary-form at the height of the Civil War, describes the nightmares and dreams of an unnamed narrator who is trapped in her apartment for two weeks because of gunshots from snipers outside.

Samman has maintained financial independence throughout her life, an uncommon situation for women of her time. She worked as a secondary school teacher when she lived in Damascus. While in Lebanon, she worked at the AUB college library before being hired as a journalist and writer for several prestigious news magazines (Sollars 696). After she completed her MA, she moved to London in order to work as a journalist and obtain a Ph.D., a project she would eventually abandon and instead devote her life to writing.

The three years Samman spent in London (1966-1969) were the

most difficult of her life and yet the most impactful in shaping her identity, her outlook on life, and her writing. Samman learned that her father died while she was in London. Also during this time, the Syrian government sentenced her in absentia to three-months in prison for leaving the country without official permission, and her Syrian relatives abandoned her because they believed her independent lifestyle made her "a fallen woman" (qtd. in Vinson). In his book *Ghada Samman bila Ajniha (Ghada Samman without Wings)*, Ghali Shukri interviews Samman who describes those formative years as follows:

> 'I stood truly alone in this fierce world, facing all the forces that were against me. … I spent [those years] … between Lebanon and various European countries, working and living like any young man alone. These years are what formed me … During those years I confronted others as a foreigner in a foreign land without the protection of family, social status, or money, and I learned what I hadn't known before. … The hardest lesson I learned was my final discovery of the superficiality of the bourgeois Damascene society that used to consider me during those years as good as dead – 'a fallen woman' – whereas I was in reality a woman starting to live her life and an artist gaining in awareness [of life around her].' (qtd. in Vinson)

Samman eventually settled in Beirut where she married Bashir Al-Daouq, a liberal-minded Lebanese man who genuinely supported women's rights and became her true ally and companion on her path as an empowered and free Arab woman. Although the Syrian president, Hafiz al-Assad, pardoned Samman in the early seventies, she never returned to Syria because she knew that it would be impossible for her to express herself freely in a rigid society that censors writers. Her decision to remain in Beirut and ultimately become a Lebanese citizen was partly due to an inner yearning for a sense of belonging to an Arab country.

Beirut was also a place that Samman could write and express herself more freely. During the second half of the twentieth century, Beirut was called the "Paris of the Middle East" and became a central location for those seeking intellectual and cultural freedom as well as artistic expression and uncensored publishing, something that appealed to many writers, including Samman's distant cousin, the poet Nizar Qabbani. The social and political environment there allowed her to more fully explore women's rights on social, economic, and political levels.

In 1977, two years into the Lebanese Civil War, Samman became the first Arab woman writer to establish her own publishing house, Manshurat Ghada al-Samman, (Publications of Ghada al-Samman). Although her husband owned a major Beirut publishing company, Dar Al Tali'a Publishing, he encouraged Samman to establish her own press there and write without censorship. Today, Samman continues to publish her writings through this press. Samman also became one of the few Arab women writers to republish all journal, press articles, and interviews about her life experiences in a series of volumes titled *al-A'maal Ghayr al-Kamila (The Incomplete Works)*. Some of the titles in the series are *Zaman al-Hub al-Akhar (Time of Another Love)*, 1978; *Al-Qabeela Tastajwib al-Qateela (The Tribe Interrogates the Victim)*, 1981; and *Al-Bahr Uhakim Samaka (The Sea Puts a Fish on Trial)*, 1986.

After establishing her press, Samman published all her subsequent works through it and republished much of her early writings as well as coverage of her work and life because she wanted to protect her experiences and viewpoints from reediting by mainstream media or other publishing companies. She also wanted to avoid the possibility of her writing being destroyed during the Lebanese Civil War. Following a fire during the early years of the war, Samman lost many of her writings, which she ultimately recovered and republished. She eloquently explains her intention to republish her work in the introduction to her short story collection *Zaman al-Hub al-Akhar (Time of Another Love)*, 1978:

> Today I live in a city threatened by a second [civil] war
> and I don't want my writings to be burned again ...
> that is why I decided to publish them ... not so much

because I feel they're important—but because I don't want them to burn.... They are part of my past and, like any past, they should not be completely effaced. By publishing them, I will ensure they will have a home in the libraries of my Arab readers, and they will be protected from ever being destroyed. (5, our translation)

Clearly, Ghada Samman is a leader and pioneer who is courageous, farsighted, passionate, and very conscious of her readers. Her work comprises a school of thought that inspires writers in the East and West and that will continue to influence many generations to come.

Literary Achievements

Samman has produced over fifty works in a variety of genres, including short stories, novels, literary criticism, essays, and poetry, through her own press. Her writings are known around the world and have been translated into twenty languages, including English, German, French, Polish, Dutch, Spanish, Russian, Italian, Bulgarian, Mandarin, Albanian, Farsi, Hindi, Korean, Romanian, Armenian, and Yugoslavian. Available in English translation are two novels, *Beirut '75* and *Beirut Nightmares*, and her short story collection *The Square Moon*. Both *Beirut '75*, translated by Nancy Roberts, and *The Square Moon*, translated by Issa Boullata, received the University of Arkansas prize for Arabic Literature in Translation into English. Furthermore, Syracuse University Press published an English translation of Samman's important novel *The Night of the First Billion*, and Darf Publishers released *Farewell to Damascus* in 2018, both translated by Nancy Roberts.

What distinguishes Samman's novels is that they address the historical and sociocultural contexts of the Lebanese Civil War (1975–1990). In *Beirut 75*, she identifies economic injustice and social disparity as the root causes of a future conflict, which became the

Lebanese Civil War. With this work, Samman also expanded the style and structure of the Arabic novel by experimenting with a narrative style that is akin to that of Virginia Woolf's stream of consciousness. Some critics who have written about this book found it reminiscent of Honoré de Balzac's *Lost Illusions* and Gustave Flaubert's *Sentimental Education* in that Beirut, like Paris, transforms into a city of madness, corruption, and death (Sollars 697).

Further, Samman's 1976 horror fantasy novel, *Beirut Nightmares,* is ranked among the top ten of the best hundred Arab novels selected by the Arab Writers Union.* Her 1986 war trilogy, *The Night of the First Billion,* is set in 1982 Geneva, Switzerland, during the time of Israel's occupation of Lebanon. The novel blends fantasy with the horrors of war to expose the atrocities of violence and the effects it has on Arab women and men. The novel skillfully blends social injustice, gender inequality, national identity, immigration issues, and cultural assimilation through the experiences of characters who manage to escape Lebanon only to find themselves alienated and challenged by a foreign and an unfamiliar culture. Overall, her novels provide a broader understanding of not only the war but also its culturally and historically specific effects on the people of Lebanon.

Samman has written ten Arabic poetry books that also address war and its intersection with love, women's rights, and cultural identity:

- *Hubb* (*Love*), 1973
- *Ashhadu 'Aksa al-Rrih* (*I Certify Against the Winds*), 1978
- *I'tikal Lahzah Haribah* (*Capturing a Fleeting Moment*), 1979
- *Al-Hubb Mina al-Wareed Ila al-Wareed* (*Love from Artery to Artery*), 1980
- *A'shiqa fi Mahbarah* (*A Lover in an Inkwell*), 1995
- *Rasa'il al-Hanin il-al-Ysamin* (*Love Letters to Jasmine*), 1996
- *Al-Abadiyyah Lahzet Hubb* (*Eternity Is a Moment of Love*), 1999
- *Al-Raqs ma' al-Boom* (*Dancing with the Owl*), 2003

---

* "The Best 100 Arabic Novels (According to the Arab Writers Union)," ArabLit, Arabic Literature and Translation (blog), M. Lynx Qualey, ed., April 23, 2010, https://arablit. org/2010/04/23/the-best-100-arabic-books-according-to-the-arab-writers-union-1-10/

- *Al-Habib al-Iftirady (The Virtual Lover)*, 2005
- *A'shikata al-Hurriya (A Woman in Love with Freedom)*, 2011

Many of these poems have been translated into English and can be found in journals, magazines, and anthologies such as *Al Jadid Magazine* and Nathalie Handal's *The Poetry of Arab Women: A Contemporary Anthology*. Samman's poetry is widely read in the Arab world and the Middle East, and her poetry books are available in Farsi, French, German, and English. Her poetry collection *Al-Abadiyyah Lahzet Hubb (Eternity Is a Moment of Love)* has been translated into English as *Arab Women in Love and War: Fleeting Eternities* by Rim Zahra in collaboration with Razzan Zahra. The poetry collection addresses the Civil War by using the erotic as a way to expose patriarchal ideologies and socio-political corruption affecting Lebanon.

This intersection between war and the erotic is a recurring theme in *Capturing Freedom's Cry: Arab Women Unveil Their Heart*, published in 1979 and originally entitled *I'tikal Lahzah Haribah (Capturing a Fleeting Moment)*. Written in the early stages of the Civil War in Lebanon (1975-1977), the book beautifully weaves together a series of poems that introduce the reader to women narrators exploring the possibilities for freedom and love within the constraints of Arab culture. Samman believes women have inalienable autonomy over their bodies and that sexuality is a necessary part of the social revolution and change in Lebanon (and in all of the Arab world for that matter). In an interview with Ghali Shukri, author of *Ghada Samman without Wings*, Samman states:

> 'It's not a secret that I have come to believe that the sexual revolution ... is an inseparable part of the Arab individual's revolution to snatch the rest of his/her freedoms ... Economical, political and the freedom of speech, of writing and thinking. There is no other salvation save the struggle against all our various concepts including our sexual concepts and the struggle against the superficial bourgeois concepts of freedom.' (qtd. in El-Hage 194)

Samman has received much critical acclaim for her work and is a highly celebrated Arab woman writer. There are twenty-one critical books about her work published in numerous languages including English, French, Russian, and Farsi. There are also many journal articles and dissertations that focus on her writing. In March 2010, the AUB celebrated Samman's achievements in a literary festival and chose her as one of sixty highly renowned alumni authors and honored her in a formal ceremony ("AUB"). Samman also received a literary award for creativity from the president of Lebanon for her 1973 short story collection *Raheel al-Marafi' al-Qadeemah* (*The Departure of Old Ports*), in which she portrays the internal conflicts among Arab intellectuals and reveals the contradictions between their beliefs and their actions ("Fifty Books" 15). The Syrian writer Fatina Saleh Kurdy describes Samman's work as a gift to the Arab world and any Arab seeking a path of freedom and empowerment. Kurdy writes:

> 'Ghada Samman left her country to pursue the dream of freedom, integrity, and self-sustenance. And she persevered with her legendary courage in the face of a traditional and harsh society. Her work has signaled a change in addressing the freedom of Arab women—a constant concern of hers and one of her most intellectual and literary contributions.' (qtd. in "Fifty Books" 15–16, our translation)

Samman's advocacy for women's autonomy and sexual freedom, particularly in traditional Arab cultures, is courageous and revolutionary, to say the least. While Samman's primary focus is on women's personal and social freedom, she believes that both Arab men and women are oppressed by patriarchy and that they should collaborate together in order to attain their freedom. The reason she gives special emphasis to women's rights is because she views them as doubly oppressed.

Some critics have recognized that, despite the feminist nature of Samman's writing, she does not write against men, but sees the possibility of men becoming women's allies in their struggle towards freedom and social and economic justice. In her narratives, the men are invited to explore alternative ways to relate to women that challenge normalized behavior. Samman depicts women's longing for men to move beyond patriarchal thought, gender ideologies, and social conditioning, and instead strive to become women's companions, friends, lovers, and allies. The Egyptian literary critic Ghali Shukri describes Samman as a supporter of freedom and human rights for the individual Arab regardless of gender when he says, "'If Naguib Mahfouz is the classical writer for Arab readers, then Ghada Samman is the first and most prominent writer for the new Arab generation.'" (qtd. in "Fifty books" 15, our translation)

Many of the poems in *Capturing Freedom's Cry* show the patriarchal nature and sexual dichotomy of relationships between men and women. They invite readers to question normalized misogynistic behavior by revealing how political and social norms and morals work in favor of men and make it almost impossible for Arab women to claim their autonomy. The poems are also a call for Arab women to claim their personal power and speak their truth, to stop hiding, stop judging and criticizing themselves, and to answer freedom's call.

The women in these poems repeatedly refuse to shy away from fulfilling their sexual longings and experiencing pleasure. They are willing to be vulnerable, to take risks with their hearts, and to dream of an idealized lover—regardless of how unattainable those dreams may be. They feel entitled to their rights to explore different sexual partners and to unashamedly express sexual desire, sexual appetite, and sexual fantasies. At the same time, these female narrators understand the patriarchal attitudes toward love that confine and limit women's freedom. They are aware of the risk they are taking when falling in love.

Yet they also know the heart is resilient in its capacity to let go and heal its wounds. When dreams are shattered, when the love spell is broken, or when they are caught in love's trap, they must find the courage to escape. They must trust their own inner strength, their ability to grow their wings and fly again. For these women, freedom is their passion, tenderness is their longing, love is their obsession, and resilience is their identity.

Samman's poems not only reflect her own personal journey into empowerment, but also reveal her belief in the relationship between the personal and the political, between women's freedom and the nation's freedom. Samman's literary achievements, life experiences, and success provide Arab women with a roadmap to navigate their own sense of freedom from a personal, intellectual, social, and political lens.

WORKS CITED

Primary Works

Ghada Samman's Works

A'inak Qadari (I Declared Love on You). Beirut: Dār al-Ādāb, 1962.

Lā Baḥr Fī Bayrūt: Qiṣaṣ (There Is no Sea in Beirut). Beirut: Dār al-Ādāb, 1965.

Layal al Ghuraba (Nights of Nostalgia). Beirut: Dār al-Ādāb, 1965.

Hubb (Love). Beirut: Ghada al-Samman Publications, 1973.

Ashhadu 'Aksa al-Rrih (I Certify against the Wind). Beirut: Ghada al-Samman Publications, 1978.

Al-A'maal Ghayr al-Kamila (Incomplete Works): Zaman Al-Hub Al-Akhar (Time of Another Love), vol. 1. Beirut: Ghada al-Samman Publications, 1978.

I'tikal Lahzah Haribah (Capturing a Fleeting Moment). Beirut: Ghada al-Samman Publications, 1979.

Al-Hubb Mina al-Wareed ila al-Wareed (Love from Artery to Artery). Beirut: Ghada al-Samman Publications, 1980.

Al-A'maal Ghayr al-Kamila (Incomplete Works): Al-Qabeela Tastajwib Al-Qateela (The Tribe Interrogates the Victim), vol. 12. Beirut: Ghada al-Samman Publications, 1981.

Al-A'maal Ghayr al-Kamila (Incomplete Works): Al-Bahr Uhakim Samaka (The Sea Puts a Fish on Trial), vol. 13. Beirut: Ghada al-Samman Publications, 1986.

Ghurbah taht al-Sifr (Nostalgia under Zero). Beirut: Ghada al-Samman Publications, 1986.

Beirut '75: A Novel. Translated by Nancy N. Roberts. Fayetteville: University of Arkansas Press, 1995.

A'shiqa fi Mahbarah (A Lover in an Inkwell). Beirut: Ghada al-Samman Publications, 1995.

Rasa'il al-Hanin il-al-Ysamin (Love Letters to Jasmine). Beirut: Ghada al-Samman Publications, 1996.

Beirut Nightmares. Translated by Nancy N. Roberts. London: Quartet Books, 1997.

The Square Moon: Supernatural Tales. Translated by Issa J. Boullata. Fayetteville: University of Arkansas Press, 1998.

Al-Abadiyyah Lahzet Hubb (Eternity Is a Second of Love). Beirut: Ghada al-Samman Publications, 1999.

Al-raqs ma' al-Boom (Dancing with the Owl). Beirut: Ghada al-Samman Publications, 2003.

The Night of the First Billion: A Novel. Translated by Nancy N. Roberts. Syracuse, NY: Syracuse University Press, 2005.

Al-Habib al-Iftirady (The Virtual Lover). Beirut: Ghada al-Samman Publications, 2005.

Arab Women in Love and War: Fleeting Eternities. Translated by Rim Zahra. Charleston, SC: BookSurge, 2009.

A'shikata al-Hurriya (A Woman in Love with Freedom). Beirut: Ghada al-Samman Publications, 2011.

Farewell to Damascus. Translated by Nancy N. Roberts. London: Darf Publishers Ltd, 2018.

Secondary Sources

"AUB to Celebrate the Works of 60 of Its Alumni Authors in a Literary Festival." *Al Bawaba*, March 9, 2010, *ProQuest Central*.

DeLamotte, Eugenia C., Natania Meeker, and Jean F. OBarr. *Women Imagine Change: A Global Anthology of Women's Resistance from 600 BCE to Present.* New York: Routledge, 1997.

El-Hage, George Nicolas. *Beirut '75 by Ghada al-Samman: An Autobiographical Interpretation.* Kindle ed., CreateSpace Independent Publishing Platform, 2017.

"Fifty Books in Novels, Short Stories, Poetry, and Travel Literature by Ghada Samman." *Al-Hassad,* no. 53 (February 2016), pp. 14–17.

Handal, Nathalie. *The Poetry of Arab Women: A Contemporary Anthology.* New York: Interlink, 2001.

Shukri, Ghali. *Ghada Samman bila Ajnihah (Ghada Samman without Wings).* Beirut: Dar al Tali'ah, 1990.

Sollars, Michael D. *The Facts on File Companion to the World Novel: 1900 to the Present.* New York: Facts on File, 2008.

Vinson, Pauline Homsi. "Ghada Samman: A Writer of Many Layers." *Al jaded Magazine,* vol. 8, no. 39 (spring 2002). www.aljadid. com/content/ghada-samman-writer-many-layers. Accessed July 20, 2017.

Wayne, Tiffany K. *Feminist Writings from Ancient Times to the Modern World: A Global Sourcebook and History.* Santa Barbara: Greenwood Press, 2011.

TRANSLATORS' ACKNOWLEDGMENT

The translators of this book, Rim Zahra and Razzan Zahra, would like to thank Ghada Samman, the author of these poems, for supporting this project and trusting in our ability to do justice to her work while translating from Arabic to English. Her welcoming response to our request to translate *Capturing Freedom's Cry* gave us a strong incentive to bring this culturally important text to an English-speaking audience. Her willingness to answer our questions while we were translating the text and writing the accompanying materials was an invaluable and treasured support. It is our goal to share her poetic, feminist vision with all those seeking to speak bravely and openly about freedom, sexuality, and oppression.

A special thanks to Dr. Helen Dunn, emeritus English professor, Sonoma State University, for stepping into the role of an English language editor and advisor. Her generous feedback throughout the translation process played a crucial role in making this translation accessible to an English-speaking audience. Her admiration for Samman's poems and her strong belief in the power of her poetry have been invaluable in shaping our choices about the semantics, syntax, and language of the poems. Our most sincere gratitude goes to her.

We would also like to thank our mom, Fatina Rashash, for her loving support and exquisite Mediterranean cuisine which made the final stages of translating this book feel effortless. The taste and aroma of her dishes awoke within us nostalgic memories of our visits to Lebanon. A special thanks to our father, Ihsan Zahra, for encouraging our education and academic accomplishments and for sharing his

147

.ories and experiences that provided insight into key historical .oments in Lebanon, Syria, Egypt, and other parts of the Arab Middle East.

We especially dedicate this translation to our aunts, grandmothers, and great-grandmothers who sought freedom within the social constraints of their times. Their struggles for freedom and desire for knowledge paved the way and inspired our passion to translate this invaluable work of art.

TRANSLATORS' BIOGRAPHIES

Rim Zahra, Ph.D., is a professor of English at Sonoma State University, Rohnert Park, California. Fully bilingual in Arabic and English, Rim is the translator of Ghada Samman's poetry collection entitled *Arab Women in Love and War: Fleeting Eternities* (2009). Rim holds a B.A. in English from the Faculty of Arts in Damascus, Syria, where she was born and grew up. She moved to Sonoma County, California, in 1999 to obtain her M.A. in English literature at Sonoma State University and then a doctorate in education at the University of California, Davis.

Rim fell in love with the collection of poems translated in this book after reading "Capturing a Lost Kiss," which drew her deeper che fierce honesty and raw intimacy of Samman's poetry. It became .ear to her that this poetry collection is invaluable in unveiling the ways women's autonomy, sexual empowerment, and ownership of their bodies are inherently tied to political manipulation and patriarchal power. Samman's frank yet lyrical treatment of war and the erotic inspired Rim to translate this collection and share its poignancy and timeless message with a larger English-speaking audience.

Razzan Zahra, Ph.D., is currently a professor of English at Sonoma State University, Rohnert Park, California, and formerly a professor of English and sociology at Phoenix University, California. There, she also served as Faculty Lead Area Chair and Campus Faculty Assessment Liaison for the College of Humanities and Sciences. Razzan is fully bilingual in both Arabic and English and contributed to the Ghada Samman's poetry translation entitled *Arab Women in Love and War: Fleeting Eternities* (2009).

Razzan was born and grew up in Damascus, Syria, where she attained her B.A. in English literature and worked as an ESL language instructor at the American Language Education Center, which she co-founded with her sister Rim. She then moved to California in 1999 to pursue her M.A. in English literature at Sonoma State University and her Ph.D. in education at the University of California, Davis. Razzan believes Samman's work has the capacity to impact a worldwide feminist audience—providing a powerful voice for women and their experience of war's realities. She herself felt transformed and empowered by Samman's poetry through the experience of translating her work because of the way Samman speaks up against the tyranny of war and the ravages of love.

Printed in the United States
By Bookmasters